MW00943276

Tango Lover's Guide to Buenos Aires

Insights and Recommendations

Migdalia Romero, PhD

iUniverse, Inc.
New York   Bloomington

Tango Lover's Guide to Buenos Aires
Insights and Recommendations

iUniverse books may be ordered through booksellers or by contacting:

iUniverse
1663 Liberty Drive
Bloomington, IN 47403
www.iuniverse.com
1-800-Authors (1-800-288-4677)

Because of the dynamic nature of the Internet, any Web addresses or links
contained in this book may have changed since publication and may no longer
be valid.

ISBN: 978-1-4401-6675-4 (sc)
ISBN: 978-1-4401-6676-1 (ebk)

Printed in the United States of America

iUniverse rev. date: 3/2/2010

DEDICATION

This book is dedicated to my father, Mario Esteban Romero, and the legacy he left me: a passion for tango. He has been with me every step of my journey. His love of tango inspired me; His knowledge of tango informed me, but it also pushed me to want to know more. And the more I got to know tango, the more I got to know my father, and the closer I felt to him. This journey has been my way of keeping daddy alive and present in my life, even though he died years before I started dancing.

Contents

Acknowledgments

I want to thank the *milongueros* who made my journey into their world so very enriching. Many gave of their time and shared information without expecting any form of remuneration. They did so out of their love of tango. Thank you, Osvaldo and Coca, Pedro and Graciela, and Gonzalo and Roxana.

I also want to thank the friends I made in Buenos Aires during my long stays. They were there for me, explaining behaviors and protocols I did not always know or understand. They introduced me to neighborhoods, restaurants, *milongas*, and events I would have missed because the regular tourist guides did not advertise them. They let me into their homes and lives, and shared traditions and perspectives that enlightened me. Thank you, Nestor, Betty, Nora, Antonio, Carlos, Marta, and Susana.

A special thanks to Jan LaSalle, Kai Cheung, and Karina Romero for their generosity in allowing me to use their photos in this guide.

Thank you, Michael, for opening up the world of tango in New York to me and for encouraging me early on to pursue the writing of this book.

I am grateful to my friends in New York who shared observations they had made during their trips to Buenos Aires, and who provided me with insights and recommendations that enriched this book. Thank you, Beverly and Jeff, Jan and Jai, Angie, Hanmi, Nancy, and Hector.

Thank you, Danel and Maria, my first tango teachers. You encouraged and pushed me from the beginning of my tango journey. In your class, you created a community of learners, students who supported each other. Thank you, Ralph, Victor, Jim, Nick, Joe, Nora, and Kathy.

Thank you, Marco, for our long conversations and your insights into the dance that have made me think about movement in new ways. And thank you for practicing with me and being honest, even to a fault.

I am also grateful to those friends who took the time to read my manuscript at different stages of development and who encouraged me to write. Thank you, Nancy, Angie, Susan, Yvonne, and Marco.

Thanks to Michelle, my cousin, who after reading the introduction said to me, "Write, write, write the book—be unstoppable." Her words sat on my desk to remind me of my mission and her belief in my project.

But most of all, I am grateful to my daughters, Sumita and Lari, for their support of my obsession, even when it took me away from them for long periods of time.

Preface

To the truly obsessed, all of what is tango is important. Certainly the dance and the dancers, but to no lesser degree the music, the song, the culture, the history, even the word. Your eye seems to find that word, wherever it appears, or perhaps it is the word that finds your eye, for it seems to leap right off the printed page.

TANGO.

Michael Purnhagen
From "Obsession"
in *La Posta del Tango*
Winter 1996

My connection to tango began as a child. My passion for tango evolved as a woman.

As a child growing up in New York, I can remember my father playing guitar and singing tangos, especially the tangos of Carlos Gardel, the tango icon of the 1920s and 1930s. Daddy had taught himself to play guitar while growing up in Puerto Rico and his choice of music was the result of the growing international popularity of Gardel, who had visited Puerto Rico in 1935 as part of a Latin American tour. My father's connection to the music, his expression, and the intensity with which he played and sang still resonate with me. I have inherited daddy's record collection, but more importantly, I have inherited his passion. There are tangos that to this day bring tears to my eyes.

Years after my father's death, I discovered *tango salon*, the dance of the people. I had seen stage tango and was moved, but not the way social tango moved me. It filled me with emotion. It inspired me. And finally, it completely overwhelmed me. This I could do, but more importantly, this I needed to do. That was the beginning of my affair and obsession with tango. It is an affair that has brought me to Buenos Aires many times, and over the course of many years.

In fact, I would have to say that tango lyrics brought me closer to my dad. They helped me to understand him better after death than while he was alive. His nostalgia for the country he left behind, his loyalty to friends, and his use of drinking to drown disappointment are all strong themes in the tango, and they were strong themes in my father's life. He dreamed of one day visiting the birthplace of tango. I finally realized my father's dream years after his death.

On my first trip to Buenos Aires more than ten years ago, I floundered for a few days, maybe even a week, without any idea of what to do first, where to go to dance, to eat, to improve my tango. I was on overload with more magazines and lists of *milongas* than I could absorb. I did not know where to begin, where to study, nor with whom, where to dance, nor where to buy shoes. There were too many choices. I was there for only four weeks and one week of that time was spent trying to get my bearings. The rest of the time was spent trying to do everything and go everywhere at a frenetic pace.

More recently, I was able to stay in Buenos Aires for almost a full year. This trip was different from previous trips in many ways. It was the realization of a lifelong dream to live in another country and to get to know its people, its language (the Spanish variety spoken in Buenos Aires), and its culture, intimately. It allowed me to do so through immersion in the culture of tango. I observed behaviors at the dance halls that no one ever taught me. I savored tango. I ate, breathed, and dreamed tango. If I was a tango aficionado before, I was now a tango junkie.

During that year, I experienced intense exposure to tango music and lyrics. I talked to old *milongueros*, i.e., men who were raised on tango, dancing it from a very young age. They helped me understand and appreciate the traditions and rituals associated with the dance. I made friends with individuals and families entrenched in tango. The movies, concerts, and restaurants I often selected fed my passion and thirst for tango even more intensely. I did it all at a leisurely pace, one that allowed me time to savor the world of tango in Buenos Aires. I returned one year later and stayed for an additional three months in order to verify and update my recommendations. My most recent trip in 2009 enabled me to note changes in the tango scene and put closure on my recommendations.

In effect, this book is the documentation of a journey. It represents and shares with its readers all that I learned exploring the secrets and intricacies of the tango culture in Buenos Aires, as a single woman traveling alone. I discovered secrets of the dance, corners of the city that sing tango, out of the way theaters that feature tango, dance clubs (*milongas*) where there were no tourists, inexpensive clothing stores that unknowingly sold clothing suited for tango, and so much more.

This book is intended for tango aficionados who want to see, feel, and hear tango at every turn and at every corner. To that end, the book is divided into seven chapters. They are as follows:

1. Preparing for your Tango Odyssey
2. Dining with Tango
3. Studying Tango
4. Dancing Tango (*Milongueando* in Buenos Aires)
5. Learning about Tango: Entertainment and History
6. Shopping for Tango
7. Tango Resources by Neighborhoods (*Barrios*)

The book is sprinkled with advice for individuals traveling alone or with a partner, without the support of an organized tour. It is written for independent travelers who want to immerse themselves in the tango scene in Buenos Aires and to take full advantage of the tango resources of this undisputed mecca of tango.

Women, especially, need a plan. It is easy for them to take the path of least resistance and to stay in their comfort zone without exploring all the richness and diversity of venues for tango that the city has to offer. However, choosing options outside of one's comfort zone can lead to wonderful surprises and opportunities for growth. More importantly, it can lead to a new appreciation of not just the dance form, but the culture of tango.

To prepare the reader for immersion in Spanish, particularly Argentinean Spanish, the book has been sprinkled with the translation into Spanish of key words and expressions. The Spanish word generally appears in parenthesis and italics right after the word in English. The words were chosen to facilitate daily interaction and comprehension of basic Spanish when eating, shopping, dancing, or taking tango classes.

Finally, the book represents a point in time (2008–2009). It does not pretend to be the last word. It encourages feedback and recommendations that emanate from the reader's experiences in Buenos Aires. In addition, it was not written to replace your regular travel guides to this city, but rather to accompany them. To that end, other tango guides are listed at the end of this book as Addendum 1.

The *Tango Lovers Guide to Buenos Aires* is dedicated to those lovers of tango music and dance, who see in Buenos Aires a mecca, a retreat, and the realization of a dream—not just a destination. It is dedicated to the self-proclaimed *milonguero* and *milonguera* who cannot miss an opportunity to dance and listen to the music, and to find out what gives this music such power and control over those who dare cross its threshold.

Chapter 1
Preparing for Your Tango Odyssey

I have spent more than one and a half of the past four years living in Buenos Aires (BsAs). I was fortunate enough to be able to live there nine months one year. Most of the time I chose to travel alone. During that time, my planning and packing were streamlined, to the point of extreme efficiency. I packed as much as I needed, used most of what was packed, and even created room for purchases made in BsAs. On the day I arrived, I immediately picked up the essential resources to know what was going on in the tango world, and by that evening or the next day I was dancing. This chapter is intended to share what I learned in order to minimize your packing, and maximize your first few days in the city so that more time is spent doing what you are going to BsAs for—dancing! This is especially important when your vacation time is limited.

OVERVIEW

To assist you in planning, this chapter is divided into four sections. The first talks about the preparation for your trip from home, from deciding how and when to go, to packing your bags. The second section provides you with an orientation to the city, focusing on how to get around BsAs and to the tango venues and resources the city offers. A third section discusses what to do on your first day(s) so as to maximize your tango experience. Finally, the chapter talks about how to manage your money and how to stay connected with the outside world, while avoiding accidents and incidents that could interfere with your tango journey.

WHAT TO DO FROM HOME

Getting to Buenos Aires

On more than one occasion, I have had the good fortune of traveling to BsAs for free, i.e., by using miles accumulated on one of my credit cards, and sometimes buying a few thousand miles to complete the trip. That combination saved me a few hundred dollars. I have also tried to minimize my cost by flying off-season (from January to June or August to November).

There are a number of ways to plan your trip. Depending on your comfort zone, you may want to go it alone for maximum freedom, or go with a friend who shares your passion for tango and your other interests. Finally, there is the option of going as part of an organized tour or a festival, preferably one that allows you some time to explore tango venues on your own.

• Traveling alone or with a friend

I have always opted to travel alone. It certainly is more challenging, and can be a bit daunting, but for me it is more satisfying. Traveling alone allows you to come and go when and where you please. It means, however, that you must have a plan. This book will help you formulate that plan.

• Tango tours organized from home

Another possibility is participating in a tango tour planned by teachers in the U.S. or in your country of origin. Tango tours provide safety, translations, planned lessons, tours, *milongas*, and day trips. However, they often lock you into the organizer's agenda, potentially limiting your opportunity to meet and socialize with the locals: *milongueros*[1] *porteños*[2]. If you are more comfortable having someone else plan your time and negotiate the language and culture for you, a tango tour is the way to go. Be sure you take it with someone who has experience, and who has successfully organized such tours in the past.

- **Tango festivals organized by the Argentinean government**

Depending on your experience and comfort level with tango, you may be more interested in participating in one of the many tango festivals that the government sponsors. Organizers generally know their city and the tango scene well and attention is usually paid to attracting relatively equivalent numbers of men and women. However, tango festivals and tours are to be avoided if you are interested in dancing only with *porteños*, or if you do not want to be part of a tourist pack.

There are both advantages and disadvantages to either traveling independently or as part of a tour group. You need to decide what is most comfortable for you.

When traveling alone or when you need to make your own flight arrangements, these are a few sources I have used that offer reasonable fares:

Consolidators: The New York Times and other newspapers often advertise low fares though agencies serving as consolidators. Their ads usually appear in very small print within the travel section of the Sunday paper.

---

1   A lover of tango as a dance form; someone who frequents the *milongas,* where tango is danced, and who is obsessed with the dance. One tango great said that the title "*milonguero*" is one that is bestowed on a man by his peers, rather than by self-appointment.

2   A man who comes from the port city of Buenos Aires.

Local Spanish newspaper ads: Newspapers such as *El Diario, La Prensa*, and other Spanish language newspapers that serve large Hispanic communities throughout the U.S. often advertise competitive airfares.

Travel agencies: Look for agencies in areas of a city that serve large South American communities, since they sometimes offer special airfares.

When to Go

I have experienced all four seasons in Buenos Aires. For me, there is no bad season. Each season has its own beauty. Winters are generally mild (compared to New York) and damp; spring and fall are delightful, and summer can be hot and humid. However, since many dance clubs are air-conditioned, the heat and humidity are manageable.

In addition, each season has its own festivals or tango-tourist draws. There are yearly scheduled international championship competitions, world tango festivals, and ongoing tango celebrations and birthdays. And then there are spontaneous tango events. The city reeks with tango.

Your decision about when to go may be determined by your vacation schedule, the season that attracts you, or your desire to participate in a special tango event or tour. Actually, anytime works since you can hear, see, and dance tango in BsAs twenty-four/seven, twelve months of the year. There is no real down time within the tango world, but there are peaks that seem to attract more tourists and thereby result in more crowded dance halls and clubs.

• Seasons

Because Argentina is in the southern hemisphere, seasons are reversed from those in the northern hemisphere.

Winter (*invierno*) runs from June 21st to September 20th. It is relatively mild (compared to U.S. winters in the north), with some chilly days and even chillier nights. Temperatures range from 40° to 64°F (5°–18° C). The winter of 2007 was particularly nippy, augmented by high levels of humidity, which in colder weather makes the cold feel colder. However, the winter days were interspersed with warmer weather and drier days. Snow is almost unheard of in BsAs. In one hundred years, there have been two snowfalls, the most recent being in the winter of 2007.

Spring (*primavera*) runs from September 21st through December 20th with temperatures ranging from 55° to 85° F (13°–29° C).

Summer (*verano*) runs from December 21st till March 20th with temperatures between 62°–95° F (17°–35° C) and often accompanied by high humidity.

Fall (*otoño*) runs from March 21st through June 20th with temperatures from 44°–72° F (7°–22° C).

• Vacation time in BsAs

January is vacation month in BsAs, when many *porteños* (as Argentineans from BsAs are called) leave the city for vacation. However, given the state of the economy, more *porteños* are staying home. Nevertheless, it is their summer. As a result, *milongas* may be slightly less crowded, an advantage for dancers who like to move around the floor.

- **Special Tango Events**
  Be sure to search the Web for special events that are going on in the world of tango in BsAs. Three good Web sites are:

> http://www.traveltango.com.ar/english/arg/
> arg/inicio_arg_eng.htm (An English Web
> site dedicated to tango.)

> http://www.bue.gov.ar (A Spanish Web
> site that provides information and links to
> services (*servicios*), including places to stay
> (*donde alojarse*) and to activities (*actividades*)
> related to tango. There is also a link on
> the home page to PDF guides for tourists
> (*extranjeros)* in ten different languages (*guía
> para extranjeros in diez idiomas*).)

> http://www.tangobuenosaires.gob.ar/   (A
> Spanish Web site prepared by the Minister
> of Culture. It contains events specific to
> tango for the current month).

Some regularly scheduled events are as follows:

> **February/March**: Tango festival (*Festival
> Buenos Aires Tango)*

> **May–June**:   Metropolitan   tango
> championship competitions *(Campeonato
> Metropolitano de Tango)* held throughout the
> city at different *milongas*.

> **Mid–August**: World tango championship
> competitions (*Campeonato Mundial de Tango*)
> for Tango Salón and Stage Tango (*Tango*

Escenario). This is a ten-day event in which many countries from around the world send their best representatives to compete in either of the two categories.

October: Tango festival

End of November – beginning of December: Bailemos Tango Festival (http://www.bailemostango.com)

December 11: National Tango Day (*Día Nacional del Tango*) features free tango concerts, performances, and guided tours throughout the city beginning in the morning. The day commemorates the birth of Carlos Gardel, the national icon of tango, and Julio De Caro, another tango great. Throughout the day there are many overlapping indoor and outdoor opportunities to hear tango and to dance—mostly for free.

Where to Stay

This section touches on your choice of housing, in terms of types of lodging and location. For those who want to dance seven nights a week and until the wee hours of the morning, the overriding concern in selecting a place to stay should be safety and easy access to the BsAs tango scene. The recommendations made in this guide are not meant to compete with or replace your standard travel guides that cover Buenos Aires lodging in depth for the general traveler. (See Addendum 1 for a listing of travel guides to Buenos Aires.)

You may start your search for lodging by Googling "hotels in Buenos Aires, Argentina," or by logging on to the government Web site (http://www.bue.gov.ar), clicking under "*servicios*" (services), and then "*alojamiento*"(lodging). Both will provide links for you to look at pictures of the hotels listed. Below are some suggestions for lodging and cautions for tango aficionados who often travel late at night.

•**Avenida de Mayo** is an area replete with old, nicely maintained, and moderately priced hotels that usually include breakfast. Avenida de Mayo is wide, well lit, well traveled, and centrally located with lots of commerce, especially restaurants that stay open late. This is critical, given that serious dancers may begin dancing after midnight and therefore arrive at their residences late and hungry. The Avenida de Mayo strip is near many *milongas*, and near public transportation. Many of the hotels on this strip have Web sites and pictures of their accommodations.

• It is a good idea to **stay on main avenues,** such as **Corrientes**, **Rivadavia**, **Santa Fe**, **9 de Julio**, and **Callao**; all located within easy reach of many *milongas*. While potentially noisy at night and early in the morning, when taxis fill the streets, establishments along these thoroughfares provide more safety when coming home from *milongas* late at night. They also are close to main transportation lines. Women traveling alone should ask about hotel security and access to the lobby by visitors. Preferably you would want a secure building that has someone in the lobby who oversees visitors twenty-four hours a day.

• Generally speaking, look to **stay in neighborhoods (*barrios*) near most *milongas* and near public transportation**. That includes *El Centro, Monserrat, Palermo, Barrio Norte,* and *Congreso.* Upscale areas such as *Retiro* and *Recoleta* are generally a little bit removed from public transportation. However, the cost and availability of taxis makes such neighborhoods another safe option.

• **Tango residences** are a relatively new phenomenon. These are privately owned town houses dedicated to tango visitors. In addition to lodging, they often provide access to teachers, dancing space for practice, meals, and other tourism services. These can be researched online by Googling "tango residences in Buenos Aires, Argentina."

• For longer stays, **look for apartments online** at Web sites such as **Craigslist** (http://www.buenosaires.craigslist.org), as well as in ads in the tango monthly publications, *BA Tango* and *El Tangauta*. Both will be described later in this chapter. Always ask about security and access to buildings at night, as well as proximity to *milongas*.

• A subscription to *Tangauta* will give you access to their magazine online. Log on to http://www.eltangauta.com/inicio.asp in order to initiate your subscription.

• Summer can be hot and sticky. For someone that requires air-conditioning, always ask if the AC is operative. By and large, even without AC, you will feel the breeze for which Buenos Aires (good air) is noted.

What to Pack

In order to reap the greatest benefits from your trip to BsAs, it is important to know beforehand what to expect and therefore, what to pack. In making sure that I am well prepared, I generally overpack. The criteria for overpacking is returning home with clothing you never got to wear, and at the same time, not having room in your suitcase to bring home what you purchased. Poor planning and packing has caused me to buy extra luggage on more than one trip in order to accommodate new purchases. On my first trip, it was for CDs and DVDs, and on another trip, it was for shoes.

I now pack an empty duffle bag into my suitcase to enable me to bring home the bulk items I buy. That always means shoes. The styles, colors, and prices make shoe shopping a sport in BsAs. On these same trips I almost always return home with outfits and shoes that are never worn. I find that I keep wearing my favorite items to different *milongas*. Men generally notice a well-dressed woman, but most do not really remember exactly what was worn. However, nothing takes the place of "beautiful dancing." In Chapter 3, I will discuss what beautiful dancing means in BsAs.

• Clothing

People tend to dress up for *milongas*, but within reason. While women may wear **dressy slacks**, more often they will wear **dresses and skirts**. And while some men still wear **suits**, especially traditional *milongueros*; more resort to **dressy sport**, wearing a shirt and slacks, but no tie.

During the winter (June through September), men often wear sport jackets, even if they do not wear ties. In the summer, they may wear light jackets to *milongas*, but remove them early on because of the heat. While the dress code for men has allowed for more casual wear, there is nothing more provocative for me than a well-dressed man. Overall, older men tend to dress up more than younger men. However, even old *milongueros* are less inclined to wear suits and ties, as they once were required to do. If you are a man who perspires a great deal, a change of shirt may be warranted. Given the intimacy of tango, a well-groomed, well-dressed, and well-scented man is more likely to be noticed by a woman, notwithstanding his ability on the dance floor.

As a woman, I have found that a few comfortable and dressy **skirts and tops** that can be combined easily are good packing choices, as are dresses that require no ironing and little maintenance. I also pack some **dressy slacks** to be combined with the same tops. I have found myself always returning to a few favorites, and leaving untouched my one-of-a-kind dressy options. Generally, select clothes that serve double duty, enabling you to move comfortably from an afternoon shopping spree to an early *milonga*. I have also found myself carrying a wrinkle free change of tops to enable me to move from one casual environment to a dressier event on the same night.

At the *milongas*, you will see new and trendy styles on the dance floor that will entice you to add to your wardrobe. Be prepared! It may just be in the leg wear, the jewelry, or most certainly, in the shoes. This gives shopaholics yet another opportunity to shop and bring back a new tango accessory, or to start a trend at home.

• Shoes

Bring at least three to four pairs of shoes, if you intend to purchase more while in BsAs. Start with one or two comfortable pairs of **dance shoes** to be able to dance right away: one for practice and one for going out. In addition, pack a comfortable and supportive pair of **walking shoes** to walk around the city; and possibly a comfortable and dressy pair to wear to the *milongas* before changing into your dance shoes.

Women are advised not to wear high, thin-heeled dance shoes on the streets. Sidewalks are often uneven and cracked. To avoid "falling between the cracks" and injuring your dancing feet, or ruining your high-heeled shoes, use sensible walking shoes to the *milonga* and keep your eyes down and in front of where you are stepping.

Both men and women should make room for the new shoes they are sure to buy. It is hard not to resist the selection of styles and colors available in stores throughout the city. Chapter 6 has a complete listing of stores that sell tango shoes.

11

• **Accessories**

Leave your best **jewelry** at home, but bring a few striking pieces (earrings, necklaces, or pins) that draw attention to you when you are seated and hoping to be asked to dance. You want to differentiate yourself from the sea of black tops that may dominate the *milonga*. You also want men to be able to find you easily once you sit down, if they have seen you on the dance floor. A striking neckpiece or top will force the eye of onlookers to stop and look.

Febreze spray is a good idea to refresh clothing after a night of dancing. While smoking is not permitted in clubs, many men will step outside for a smoke and carry that odor on their clothes, thereby transmitting it to you. It is also useful for refreshing the insides of your shoes.

For maintaining your shoes, a **brush** (*cepillo*) for suede (*gamusa*), and **shoe polish** (*tinta*) for leather (*cuero*) is recommended. In addition, to ensure smooth dancing even on sticky floors, bring a small case of **talcum powder**.

If you plan on dancing afternoons and nights and your feet have a tendency to swell, an **ice pack** is a good addition, as is Advil or some other **anti-inflammatory** to reduce swelling. On my first trip, I had come out of bunion surgery the year before. I went prepared with an ice pack and every night I would pamper my feet. Icing, together with an anti-inflammatory, made a big difference.

In order to read the small print of tango maps, it is a good idea to carry a pocket-sized **flashlight** and **magnifying glass**. Maps are packed with streets crisscrossing each other. Even the best of eyes struggle to see the small print, especially in a dark taxi, as you move from *milonga* to *milonga*. I have been lucky enough to have a map when the taxi driver was not sure about the route to a *milonga* that was off the beaten path. Three such *milongas* are La Baldosa, Sunderland, and Sin Rumbo. Chapter 4 has a complete review of these and other *milongas*.

Adaptors, converters, and transformers will enable you to use appliances from home. Adaptors simply change the plug configuration so that your two-prong parallel connectors from the U.S. can be used in the two round receptors that are found in BsAs. Adaptors are adequate for low voltage laptops, Ipods, and the like. Converters and transformers are used with high heat items such as hair dryers and items that require more voltage. They change the current from 240v to 120v.

Don't forget a **dictionary**. It is helpful as you try to get through material written only in Spanish, such as the newspapers or flyers. For the more adventurous traveler looking to improve their Spanish, it is essential.

• Seasonal Packing

Be aware of the season you are going into as you select clothing to bring. In addition, the varied and unpredictable winter temperatures and sudden drops in temperature at night require one to **dress in layers**. For women, that means a top layer such as a shawl, scarf, or wrap that can dress up any outer jacket, coat, or trench coat. A light, dressy jacket, sweater, or shawl can be worn over the layer you want dancers to see at a *milonga*.

In addition, **fans** for women and **handkerchiefs** for men are also used extensively to protect oneself from the heat. Some of the old time *milongueros* place a folded handkerchief in their hand while they dance in order to protect their partner from their perspiration.

HOW TO GET AROUND BsAs

You have arrived, probably on an overnight flight. You may be high on adrenaline and anxious to dance. While dancing may be your main goal, taking time to orient yourself to the city is important and in the long run may increase your dancing time. It certainly will help you get around more quickly and efficiently. Therefore, it is a good idea to settle in, walk around, and collect a few resources to make moving around the city and getting to the *milongas* a pleasurable experience.

This section will provide you with ways of getting to and from Ezeiza, the international airport, as well as an orientation to the city and the public forms of transportation that move you around the city. It will also provide you with a quick listing of neighborhoods (*barrios*) that are reflected in guides and maps, and that most heavily feature tango.

To and From Ezeiza Airport

• Bus service
Manuel Tienda Leon (http://www.tiendaleon.com). This service will cost you approximately 85 *pesos* round trip, and 45 *pesos* one-way. Tickets can be purchased at a dedicated booth at the airport. Buses take you to a central point in downtown BsAs. There you are transferred to a van that takes you to your door.

• Remis or radio-taxi
Radio-taxis are generally waiting outside the airport. For safety, you should ask the driver for his card or telephone, explaining that you may want to use his services when you return. You can expect to pay from 75 to 100 *pesos* (approximately $20–$26) one-way for door-to-door service.

Arrangements can also be made in advance for pick-up and airport drop off through some of the individuals and services that advertise in the local monthly tango magazines, *El Tangauta* and *BA Tango*. See Chapter 4 (*Milongueando* in BsAs) for more details about these publications and other tango sources, some of which are available online.

Orientation to the City

The cardinal reference point in BsAs is the *Obelisco* pictured on the right.

It is a modern monument situated in the heart of the city at the intersection of two major thoroughfares, *Av Corrientes* and *Av 9 de Julio*. The latter is a twenty-two-lane avenue that traverses the city from the southern end at *San Telmo* to the northern end at *Recoleta*.

The area surrounding *El Obelisco* is referred to as the *Centro* and it is where many tango venues can be found—from studios and schools to dance halls, clubs, tango bars, and theaters. *El Centro* is the heart of both the city and the theater district.

• **Rivadavia Avenue (*Avenida*)** divides Buenos Aires into north and south sectors. This main artery begins in the easternmost section of the city at the *Casa Rosada* (White House of BsAs) and extends far out into the provinces. Intersecting streets (*calles*) on either side of Rivadavia have different names (see Table 1). As an example, *Calle* Perú intersects Rivadavia on the south side. The extension of Perú on the north side is called *Calle* Florida. Likewise, *Calle* Tacuarí becomes *Calle* Suipacha at Av Rivadavia. Streets also begin their numbering off Rivadavia, starting at 0. For example, the 700 block of *Calle* Florida is seven blocks away from Rivadavia. The famous *milonga* La Ideal is on Suipacha 384, which means the 300 block of Suipacha, or three blocks away from Rivadavia.

Below is a summary of the streets that run on either side of Rivadavia in the heart of the city. This area is replete with *milongas*, shoe stores, shopping malls, and tango schools.

TABLE 1

Casa Rosada
EAST END

CALLE		CALLE
Leandro M Alem		Paseo Colón
25 de Mayo		Balcarce
Reconquista		Defensa
San Martín		Bolivar
Florida		Perú
Maipu		Chacabuco
Esmeralda		Piedras
Suipacha	Av Rivadavia	Tacuarí
Av 9 de Julio		Av 9 de Julio
Libertad		Salta
Talcahuano		Santiago del Estero
Uruguay		San Jose
Parana		Luis Saenz Peña
Montevideo		Virrey Cevallos
Rodriguez Peña		Solis
Av Callao		Av Entre Rios

Congreso
WEST END

Other main avenues that run through *El Centro* and that coincide with the underground transportation system (*subtes*) are as follows:

• *Avenida* **Corrientes** runs more or less parallel to, and north of, Rivadavia. *Subte* Line B runs under this important avenue. It takes you to the famous cemetery *Chacarita* at the west end, where the tango icon Carlos Gardel and other tango greats are buried.

• *Avenida* **9 de Julio** runs perpendicular to *Avenidas* Corrientes, Rivadavia, and Santa Fe. 9 de Julio is serviced by *subte* Line C. This avenue is a twenty-two-lane thoroughfare that runs from the historical San Telmo barrio at the south end, to Recoleta, the upscale residential *barrio* at the north end. As noted earlier, 9 de Julio is marked by *el obelisco* at its intersection with *Avenida* Corrientes. Both *el obelisco* and 9 de Julio are cardinal points of orientation. Within one block of the *obelisco* you will find one of the oldest and most popular tango venues, Confitería La Ideal.

• *Avenida* **Santa Fe** also runs parallel to Av Rivadavia in the downtown area, and then fans out as it moves northwest. It is serviced by *Subte* Line D. Av Santa Fe traverses more upscale shopping and residential areas.

A complete description of the *subte* system is provided later in this chapter.

The Barrios

The federal district (*Distrito Federal)* of Buenos Aires is divided into **neighborhoods (*barrios*)**. Depending on the map, the names of the *barrios* and their lines of demarcation may vary. For this book, I have included twelve *barrios*. Below they are grouped by geographic proximity. The most popular *milongas* and tango resources are clustered within the following *barrios*:

• **El Centro including Microcentro** encompasses the historical and cultural core of the city. It includes the financial district, government buildings, the theater district, and a heavily traversed commercial district. Table 1 (in the previous section) reflects *El Centro*, but the illustration also includes parts of Congreso at the western end and parts of San Telmo at the southern end.

• *Barrio* **Balvanera including Bo. Once** begins at *Av* Callao and runs west through *Av* Pueyrredón (not shown on Table 1).

• *Barrios* **Abasto, Almagro, and Boedo** run west of *Av* Pueyrredón. Some very popular *milongas* (including Gricels), as well as tango bars, *boliches*, and shoe stores can be found in these *barrios*.

• *Barrios* **Recoleta, Norte, and Palermo** are adjoining *barrios* that lie north of *Av* Santa Fe. They are noted for their high-end shopping and residences. A few *milongas* and bars/clubs that feature tango musical shows can be found in these barrios.

• *Barrios* **Monserrat, San Telmo, and La Boca** are adjoining *barrios* south of *Av* Rivadavia. A great deal of tango history was made in these *barrios*. Many buildings date back to the colonial period. San Telmo is well known for antiques, cafés, tango bars, and weekend pedestrian antique and craft fairs that also feature free tango entertainment in the streets.

• **Villa Urquiza**, while off the beaten path, hosts two of the most traditional and oldest *milongas* that should be visited as a way to be transported to another era.

Chapter 7, the last chapter of this book, will provide an orientation to the twelve *barrios*, and gather all the tango resources that can be found in each of them.

Local Transportation

• Trains (*Subte*)

Currently there are four *subte* lines (A, B, D, and E) that run somewhat parallel to each other on different avenues. Eventually, these lines fan out to cover the outlying areas that fall within the city limits. There are two additional lines (C and H) that run perpendicular to the aforementioned lines. A good Web site for an orientation to this underground system of transportation is: http://www.urbanrail.net/am/buen/buenos-aires.htm. It includes a map of the system.

The *subte* trains are very reliable, running approximately every three to four minutes during weekday rush hour, and every seven to ten minutes on weekends. They begin their runs at 5:00 or 6:00 AM. However, the lines discontinue service at 10:00 or 11:00 PM. This schedule does not serve tango aficionados who tend to dance late into the night and, more likely, until the wee hours of the morning. However, the *subte* is a good source of transportation for those shopping during the day and for getting to afternoon and early evening *milongas*. After ten or eleven, dancers must either take buses (*colectivos*) or taxis (*remis*) to get around.

You can get *subte* cards for up to ten rides for 11 *pesos*, a convenience and a good way to avoid long lines when you are in a hurry to get to a *milonga*. Single rides are 1.10. Cards for single rides or for up to ten rides are purchased at the ticket counter before going through the turnstile. For one ten-trip ticket, ask the attendant for "*una de diez.*" When swiped, the card records the day and time of your trip and the number of trips left on the card. Obviously, it must be retrieved from the turnstile for subsequent use.

The *subte* system is also very colorful. Vendors sell all kinds of goods, oftentimes leaving samples on your lap for your inspection. They then come around to complete the sale or to pick up the sample they left with you.  People are quite honest and even if riders leave the train early, they will leave the merchandise behind. Musicians and dancers may also entertain you in anticipation of some change (*monedas*).

As of May 2009, the *subte* lines were as follows:

Line A: runs east-west along *Av* de Mayo/ Rivadavia. This is the oldest line. Many of the original trains in use require passengers to slide the doors open, manually, for access, since they do not open automatically. Doors must be opened manually from inside and outside the car. If you wait for the doors to open, you will miss your stop or your ride. However, doors close automatically as soon as the train begins to move out of the station.

Line B: runs east-west along *Av* Corrientes. It runs through *Bo* Abasto, where Carlos Gardel, the tango icon, had a house that has been converted into a museum. That station is named after him. In addition, this barrio has a number of shoe stores, tango bars, tango schools, and a large shopping  mall accessible from the Gardel station.

Line C: runs north-south along *Av* 9 de Julio from El Retiro to Constitución in San Telmo. It makes connections with Lines A, B, D, and E at designated stations, allowing riders to transfer for free. It crosses the barrios of San Telmo, El Centro, and Retiro.

Line D: runs east-west along *Av* Córdoba, and then follows *Av* Santa Fe through Recoleta, Barrio Norte, and Palermo.

Line E: runs east-west along Av San Juan through *Barrios* Monserrat, Constitución, and Boedo.

Line H: the newest line inaugurated in October 2007, runs north-south along *Av* Pueyrredón, from *Av* Rivadavia at the north end to *Caseros* at the south end. It currently connects with Lines A and E. Eventually, Line H will extend to Retiro at the north end, and connect with Lines B, C, and D.

Currently the transit system is testing a public transportation debit card (monedero). It will eventually allow passengers to board all buses and trains by swiping the card on a screen. Details are available at www.monedero.com.ar.

• Buses (*Colectivos*)

The bus system in BsAs is cheap, extensive, and very reliable. Currently, there are more than 140 bus lines. Busses run around the clock, seven days a week and twenty-four hours a day. There is an inexpensive guide, *Guía-T,* enabling you to navigate the rather complex system of buses. A compact version is sold at newsstands (*kioscos*) and by street vendors on the trains. The guide is divided into three sections. The first section alphabetically lists every street in BsAs (*Calles de Capital Federal).* The second section has maps that divide every section of the city into twenty-four quadrants, indicating the bus lines that run through each quadrant (*Planos y Grilla de Colectivos).* The third and last section lists every bus line by number, and indicates the streets that the line traverses (*Recorrido de los Autotransportes de Pasajeros).*

How to use the T guide (*Guía T*) and get around by bus (*colectivo*)

A starting point is to identify the bus lines that come close to your residence. Next, look up the street and the number of the building you are going to in the front section of the T guide. Find the map it references, and the quadrant on which that street is found. Look (with a magnifying glass) for your address in the appropriate quadrant. Then look at the corresponding quadrant on the facing page to see the buses that run in that quadrant. See if there is a match between the buses that run by your residence and those that go to your destination.

At the time of writing this, bus rides were 1.10 to 1.25 cents (centavos), depending on how far you were going. You must pay with coins, but change is provided. Keep *peso* coins, i.e., coins that are valued at one dollar/*peso* since they are sometimes hard to come by. Drivers do not handle money. Riders place their coins into a metal box upon entering the bus and the same box provides change.

Once you are near the driver and next in line to pay, indicate your destination. In turn, the driver will code in the amount you have to pay and it will appear on the money box screen. My best advice is to look at the person in front of you to know exactly where the money should be placed, since the slot and even the placement of the coin box varies from bus to bus. The machine has a small screen that indicates what you have to pay, what you have put in, and when the receipt is being printed (*boleto imprimiendose*). It will also give you change and print out your receipt. Receipts should be kept for the course of the ride, in case you are asked to produce it by an inspector.

Don't be surprised if your driver suddenly re-routes the bus without warning, before picking up the regular route after a short distance. This usually occurs because of political and/or social demonstrations in the downtown area, especially around *Av* de Mayo and the *Casa Rosada*, or around the Congreso and *Av* Callao. It is helpful to carry a street map or the T guide to follow the new route.

Instructions for getting around by bus in BsAs can be found online at:

www.tripadvisor.com/Travel-g312741-c5232/Buenos-Aires:Argentina:How. To.Use.A.Public.Bus.In.Buenos.Aires. html

• Radio-Taxis and *Remises*

There are two alternatives to mass transit: radio-taxis and *remises*. Radio-taxis are metered and can be called or they can be signaled or hailed on the streets. On the other hand, *remises* (private car services) require a reservation and generally give you a flat rate determined by distance. Avoid hailing taxis that do not have a telephone number visible on the outside of their taxi, and always be sure to note the telephone of the taxi you are taking.

It is a good idea to carry small bills and change with you to pay drivers, since they do not change large bills, nor do they carry a great deal of change. Drivers usually round off the fare to the higher dollar figure. If a passenger does not have the exact fare, the driver may round out the ride to the lower round figure. For example, for a ride of 5.20 (*pesos*) I gave the driver 10 *pesos*. In return, he gave me change of 5 *pesos*.

Tipping is generally not expected. However, given the economy and the low fares, I have made an exception. I generally add an extra *peso* or two as a tip depending on the service, the fare, the distance, and the time taken. Or I may round off the fare to the higher peso amount.

Upon entering a taxi, remember to **greet the driver**, with "good day" (*buenos días* or *buenas noches*). It is an expected courtesy. It is not unusual for a driver to respond to the address you give him as your destination (without a salutation), with "*buenos días,*" said with sarcasm. At that point, I apologize, greet the driver appropriately and then repeat my address.

• Hydrofoil/Ferry (*Buquebus*) to Uruguay

If you are lucky enough to be able to stay in BsAs for more than three months you must be re-authorized to do so. You can do this by leaving Argentina, having your passport stamped in another country, and then returning to BsAs—all in a day. This can be accomplished by taking a very pleasurable trip to Colonia.

Colonia is a Spanish and Portuguese city in Uruguay, on the other side of the *Rio Plata*. You can get there in one hour by hydrofoil (high speed ferry) and in three hours by regular ferry. While the former is more expensive, both are delightful. Two and a half hours on a hydrofoil brings you to Montevideo, Uruguay, where you can also dance tango.

WHAT TO DO ON YOUR FIRST TWO DAYS

On my first trip to BsAs, I floundered around the city for more than a few days, trying to figure out the lay of the land. I was overwhelmed with options, too much information, and too little direction. All I knew was that I wanted to dance. But where should I go first? With whom should I study? Who were the best teachers? And where were the best *milongas*? What I discovered on subsequent trips is that time spent on the first day orienting myself and gathering resources paid off in the long run. This section is intended to put you on the right path the day you arrive so that you make smart choices early on. To that end, you need to spend the first twenty-four to forty-eight hours picking up the following items:

• **Tango Map:** You should pick up a tango map of the city with all regular *milongas* listed by day and numbered on the map. They are available at local tango shoe stores. For example, one block down from the *Confitería* La Ideal on the 200 block of Suipacha there are a series of shoe stores that usually carry this map. It is one of the best resources for your stay and it is free. While in the vicinity of La Ideal, stop in and pick up flyers announcing their *milongas*, guest teachers, and special shows. You may even take in a *milonga*, since dancing at La Ideal is a seven-day-a-week option, with many days starting as early as 3:00 PM.

Tango maps are also available at the tourist information center in the downtown area (*El Centro*) on the 200 block of *Calle* Florida, within walking distance of La Ideal. *Calle* Florida is a pedestrian mall that runs for about eight blocks. It is filled with stores selling clothing, shoes, leather goods, books, CDs, and souvenirs, and featuring street musicians and tango dancers.

• **Free Tango Publications** (available at many *milongas*): *Tangauta, B.A. Tango, and La Milonga* are three monthly bilingual (Sp/Eng) tango magazines (*revistas*) with articles, pictures, interviews, and lots of ads for teachers, schools, housing, clothing, shoes, and even transportation. Most importantly, there are many pages listing classes (*clases*), practice sessions (*prácticas*), workshops (*talleres*), and dances (*milongas*) organized by day and time. They also list *milongas* that feature shows (*milongas con espectáculos*), local shows, open mikes in restaurants (*cafés, concert restaurantes*, and *peñas*), and tango theater productions (*teatros*). The section in *Tangauta* labeled "LQV" ("*lo que vendrá*"), "what is coming," focuses on shows and events that are forthcoming. In *B.A. Tango,* the equivalent section is called "where to go" ("*orientación para salidas*"). One shortcoming of both publications is that they often come out late into the month. However, your *milonga* listings don't change appreciably from one month to the next. In addition, *B.A. Tango* publishes a pocket-sized tri-monthly guide to *milongas* and classes, entitled **Guía Trimestral, B.A. Tango**.

A smaller monthly guide, **Diostango**, comes out early each month. It too is free, bilingual, and contains ads, a few short articles, lots of photos, and a really handy two-page guide to *milongas*. I generally cut out these two pages and keep them in my purse for easy reference, in case the *milonga* I chose to go to that night is not very good. This publication may also be available in the tango kiosk on *Av* Corrientes 1500, the corner of Parana.

A lesser-known monthly tango publication, **La Porteña Tango,** is also available for free at some restaurants, *milongas*, and kiosks. It has excellent articles on the history of the music and musicians. However, it is written only in Spanish. The last page has a section entitled "The Tango Scene of the Month" ("*Tangomovida del Mes*"). It contains a rather comprehensive listing of shows (*espectáculos*) and tango dinner shows (*tango-cena shows*). This is a great opportunity to use your dictionary and thereby extend your Spanish.

• **Street and subway maps:** In order to get around the center of town, you should have a pocket-sized city map. *Galerías* Pacífico, a beautiful indoor shopping mall on *Calle* Florida and *Av* Córdoba, offers a handy bilingual, folded pocket-sized tourist map (*plano turístico*). It includes a small image of the underground transportation (*subte*) system.

While in the *Galería* look into the **Borges Cultural Center** around the back of the gallery, and also check out the **Argentine School of Tango**. The cultural center always offers tango entertainment and the school offers classes seven days a week. Pick up their flyers.

• **Newspapers:** *Clarín* and *La Nación* are two Spanish daily newspapers. They include an entertainment section (*"Espectáculos"*) every day. On Fridays, they contain a section focused on weekend entertainment. There is even a section on "2x4" that lists tango shows. Newspapers are another opportunity to use your dictionary, while improving your Spanish skills. If you are interested in improving your fluency, I recommend reading aloud articles that deal with subjects that interest you and with which you are familiar.

On Fridays, the **Buenos Aires Herald**, produced in English, publishes a section entitled "Getting Out". It summarizes entertainment opportunities for the week-end, including those related to tango.

Other guides and maps are available at **tourist kiosks and information centers**. One is located on the second floor of *Galerías* Pacífico, another at the 200 block of *Calle* Florida.

HOW TO MANAGE MONEY, COMMUNICATION, AND SAFETY

Managing your Money

You can print out a handy FX cheat sheet from http://www.oanda.com. It provides a quick reference to your dollar-to-peso and peso-to-dollar exchange rates. This is good to have as you pay 300 *pesos* for a pair of shoes, knowing that it may only be the equivalent of $79.00, or that 25 *pesos* for a CD is costing you only $6.57. And a train ride to a *milonga* costing 1.10, really costs around 0.27 cents. BsAs at this time is one of the best bargains in the world, even as the prices rise and inflation sets in for the *porteño*. As of 7/09, the U.S. dollar exchange was 1 USD to 3.69 *pesos*.

Staying Connected with Home

• *Locutorio:* These are businesses that allow you to make calls and use a computer at all hours. For the use of computers most *locutorios* charge anywhere from 2 to 3 *pesos* an hour. On some blocks you will find two or three *locutorios*. Computers are imported and, therefore, are a casualty of the exchange rate. As such, they are extremely expensive and not owned by the masses. That might account for the preponderance of *locutorios* throughout the city.

• **Telephone Cards:** In addition, you can purchase local and international pre-paid phone cards for very little. I always purchase both, since making either local or international calls is easier with one, especially if made from your hotel or apartment. On my most recent trip, international calling cards were available for 10 *pesos* ($2.63). I was able to call the United States and talk for up to one hour with the calling card, *Llamada Directa, Internacional.*

Telephone dialing codes

Int'l code for the United States	001
Int'l code for Argentina	54
City code for Buenos Aires	11
Telephone numbers within BsAs	8 digits
Cell phone code	15

• **Post Office:** Sending packages by UPS or another carrier is an expensive proposition. In the nine contiguous months I spent in BsAs, I purchased many shoes and found I could not accommodate their bulk easily in my luggage, which was already overflowing. I sent a box of shoes home but had to pay dearly for it. Nevertheless, it was cheaper than buying the shoes in New York, and certainly the styles and colors could never be replicated there.

• **Cell Phones:** Cell phones can be rented for the time of your stay. A number of companies provide this service. Service carriers can be found online by Googling "cell phone rental in Buenos Aires," or the rental can be obtained in BsAs at a local mobile phone store after you arrive.

Safety for Dancers

• **Wounded sidewalks:** Walking the streets of BsAs can be dangerous to a dancer, albeit a necessary and enlightening experience. The architecture and *cúpulas* (building domes) are worth looking up at. However, to avoid twisting an ankle, which would prevent you from dancing, keep your eyes on the ground, looking for cracks, holes, missing tiles, speed bumps, and uneven streets. Periodically, pull over to the side of the street to stop and look up. A short stop in the middle of a narrow and crowded thoroughfare could end up inconveniencing everyone behind you who is trying to get by.

• **Pickpockets:** As in any large city, BsAs has its fair share of petty thievery of which I have been a victim. Therefore, caution is advised. Never hang your pocketbook on the back of your chair, as I once did. When I went to pay for dinner, the bag was missing. Always keep valuables in your possession or, at least, within your vision. I also found it helpful to keep my change in a separate change purse *(monedero)*, which is especially good for use on buses.

Do not use a cell phone while walking, nor open a wallet to remove money in the middle of the street or in a crowded bus or train. Put your money away as soon as you receive change, not while you are walking on the streets. Thieves are known for preying on distracted pedestrians, even in the middle of the day and on crowded streets. They are also known for flagrantly taking and running away with things of value, such as a cell phone or a wallet.

• **Walking at night:** Avoid deserted streets at night, always choosing to walk on the main avenues where the subway lines run, e.g. *Avenida* de Mayo/ Rivadavia, Corrientes, Córdoba, *and* Santa Fe. For example *Av* Corrientes, Buenos Aires' theater district, is a twenty-four-hour thoroughfare with many restaurants, bars, movie houses, theaters, and the like. On the other hand, *Calle* Tucumán, that runs parallel to Corrientes (just two blocks away), is desolate and to be avoided at night, especially by women traveling alone.

A CLOSING NOTE

Over the course of many years and long stays in Buenos Aires, I have learned a great deal, not just about the dance, but about the people, the culture, and the city that contributes to its tango mystique. Most of all, I have learned to slow down, to listen, and to look. The more I looked, the more I saw. Each trip to BsAs was like revisiting an old treasured book that becomes dearer to you with each reading, and that over time enables you to appreciate and understand it better. You get to know the characters more intimately and you begin to notice things you had not noticed before, or you begin to make new connections between people, places, and events.

In BsAs, the more you immerse yourself in the landscape, the more you fall in love with the city. The more you walk the streets, the more you see. The more you mingle with the *Porteños*, the better you understand them. As for tango, the more you observe it, the more you notice; the more you study it, the more you realize how much there is to learn; and the more you dance it, especially with *milongueros*, the more you appreciate it. At another level, the more you listen to the music, the more you really hear.

The rest of this book will take you through the streets, into the restaurants, the studios, the clubs, the pubs, the theaters, and the shops that cater, consciously or unwittingly, to the tango frenzy that is sweeping the world and that brings more and more people to BsAs each year.

Overall, remember that the pace of life in this beautiful city is much slower than in large cities in the United States. People do not rush to eat, to get a check, or even to get places. In general, I slowed down my pace appreciably in the city. That enabled me to see more, hear and discover more, and relish every moment. Sit back and enjoy the view and do so with some abandon, albeit with caution.

Bon Voyage!

Chapter 2
Dining with Tango

I had just arrived in BsAs, and walked around my *barrio* to find a place to have lunch. I stumbled on a small *parrillada* where meat is cooked on an open grill in full view of the patrons. The walls of this little restaurant were filled with images—photos, posters, news clippings, and artwork—all related to tango. Tango music played in the background very gently. I soon discovered that the owner of this little gem, Omar Escudero, sang tango with Donato Racciati's orchestra back in the 1970s. After a few more visits and conversations with the owner, I also discovered that on Saturday nights, he and his patrons sang spontaneously, accompanied by a keyboardist—all for the price of dinner.

Personal Memoir
November 2007

OVERVIEW

This chapter begins with an overview of dining in Buenos Aires. The remainder of the chapter is divided into two parts. The first and most extensive section lists and describes restaurants that feature tango, as part and parcel of a commercial dinner show, or as an accompaniment to dinner, or just as a backdrop for dinner and drinks. The second section describes typical meals, and some of the most popular dishes and their English equivalents.

DINING IN BUENOS AIRES

Dining in BsAs offers the tango lover yet another opportunity to relish the music, while eating in places where tango seeps through the walls and fills the air.

In reality, eating in this city is more like eating in Europe than in the United States. Breakfast fare is light and dinner begins late—very late. Therefore, don't rush to eat and don't expect the check (*la cuenta*) right away. Out of respect for customers, waiters do not pressure you to leave by giving you the check unsolicited. In Argentina, you need to ask for it by signaling the waiter/waitress, the way you do in many cities around the world. You may even have to ask for the menu (*la carta, por favor*).

Enjoy the leisurely approach to eating, serving, and charging that is characteristic of this European-like city. It is not unusual to sit for breakfast in a café for an hour, drinking *café con leche*, eating small croissants (*medialunas*), and sipping freshly squeezed orange juice (*exprimido*), while reading the newspaper (*diario*). In fact, many cafés have the daily newspaper available for you to read. If the paper is on someone else's table and no one is reading it, you are permitted to ask (1) if it is their paper (*¿Es suyo?*), and (2) if you can read it (*¿Puedo verlo?*).

Meal times in BsAs are in conflict with a tango dancer's timetable and lifestyle. Generally, breakfast is served too early, especially at hotels that serve only until 10:00 AM, when some dancers are just getting up. On the other hand, dinner at many restaurants and *parrilladas* is served too late, i.e. after

9:00 PM, when dancers may just be getting ready for nighttime dancing. Besides, a heavy meal before going out to dance is not usually a good idea. The alternative at night is to eat at a café, pizzeria, or restaurant that stays open all day and offers light fare; an option that is more appropriate for dancers.

RESTAURANTS THAT FEATURE TANGO

The restaurants listed below were selected because they feature tango in a variety of ways. Some of them provide a lavish tango show, as part of the dinner menu. Others offer you the option of dining à la carte, while viewing a formal show, listening to live music, or watching dancers perform. Still others simply cloak their walls with tango memorabilia (vintage photos and news clippings, signed portraits, old playbills, or ads for tango events), as they play tango quietly in the background. They may even feature tango music and/ or dance performances one or two nights a week. All of them give you the opportunity to dine with tango, and to hear and sometimes see the protagonists of tango. A few even give the customer the opportunity to sing or dance.

Commercial Dinner Shows (Cena-tango shows)

Below is an alphabetical listing of dedicated restaurant-theaters that offer tango spectaculars, sometimes interspersed with folk music, in combination with a formal dinner (selective menus) and drinks. At some places alcoholic drinks are charged separately. Shows last from one and a half to two hours, and feature live music, singers, and dancers. In some cases, you can see the show without dinner for a reduced rate. *Cena-tango* shows are, by far, the most expensive places to see and hear tango. Generally, they represent "tango for export," the tango that foreigners expect to see and that *milongueros* avoid.

There is a less expensive and less spectacular theater dinner option that caters to locals. These establishments change their programming and guest artists weekly. The emphasis in these restaurants is on authentic music, with less attention to folklore or exhibition dancing.

Reservations at these theater-restaurants should be made in advance. You can expect to pay anywhere from 100 pesos for the dinner show to 600 *pesos* for an enhanced package that includes dinner and drinks. This is sometimes referred to as a VIP option. Substantial discounts for some of these *cena* shows are available from the discount houses (*carteleros*) on Av Corrientes:

1. *Cartelero #1*: Corrientes 1382, locale 24
2. *Cartelero #2*: Corrientes 1660, locale 2 in *Paseo de la Plaza*

The Web sites for the establishments listed below are worth opening, since a number of them provide historical information and even timelines about the evolution of tango. They also include menus, clips of their shows, as well as pictures of their interiors. Oftentimes, you can choose to view the Web site in English. However, opting for Spanish provides you with yet another opportunity to read the language of tango, while viewing images on screen. This is a great way to reinforce and extend your knowledge of Spanish.

The newspapers (*diarios*) *Clarín* and *La Nación* provide a listing of dinner shows that are open each night. Many, but not all, commercial shows are offered seven nights a week. Therefore, it is a good idea to call the theater or to check the newspaper before making plans. The "E" section entitled "*Espectáculos*" (Shows) or "*Entretenamiento*" (Entertainment) lists ads under "*Cena-tango shows*" or "*Teatro*" or "Restaurant Concerts."

Each entry in this section designates the more expensive tourist option with "$$$", if the dinner option runs over 300 pesos. If the cost is 100 pesos or less, a single "$" appears under "**Cost in *pesos***". Shows that charge between 200 and 300 pesos are marked with "$$". As a promotion, many dinner theaters run weekday specials. They are usually advertised in local newspapers. Some offer a discount for payment in cash. The "**Cost in *pesos***" indicated here was in effect October, 2009. However, given fluctuations in the economy, prices should be verified at the time that reservations are made.

Café de los Angelitos
Rivadavia 2100 (Bo. Balvanera/Congreso)
Tel: 4952-2320
http://www.cafedelosangelitos.com

The original café dates back to the 1890s. The new structure recently opened its doors as a restaurant by day and a *cena* show by night, in a separate and private section. The walls in the restaurant include pictures of the original café and of many tango protagonists. It is opened all day for light fare and pastries. On some afternoons the strains of a guitarist and/or a *bandeonista* serve as a backdrop for lunch. The restaurant has a large theatre in the back for their *cena* show.
Cost in *pesos*: $$$

Candilejas
Estados Unidos 1500 (Corner of Saenz Peña; Bo. Monserrat)
Tel: 4304-0885
http://www.candilejastango.com.ar

This restaurant is a dedicated dinner theater targeting locals, and open only on Friday and Saturday.
Cost in *pesos*: $

El Querandí
Perú 302 (Corner of Moreno; Bo. San Telmo)
Tel: 4345-0331
http://www.querandi.com.ar

El Querandí is an historic bar that dates back to 1920. It has been restored as a dinner theater, offering a tango show that traces tango from its early bordello roots when men practiced together, to stage tango as it is danced in theaters. The restaurant is open Monday through Sunday; dinner begins at 8:30 PM followed by the show at 10:15 PM.

Cost in *pesos*: $$$

El Viejo Almacén
Balcarce 799 (Corner of Independencia; Bo. San Telmo)
Tel: 4307-7388
http://www.viejo-almacen.com.ar/

Although the current establishment dates back to only 1969, it is entrenched in a great deal of tango history. It is located in the heart of San Telmo on a cobblestone street, surrounded by many historic buildings and small café-restaurants. A tango entitled El Viejo Almacén was written in 1924 and can be heard on its Web site. The restaurant offers a pre-fixe lunch, and a few dinner-show options.

Cost in *pesos*: $$

Esquina Carlos Gardel
Pje. Carlos Gardel 3200 (Corner of Anchorena; Bo. Abasto)
Tel: 4867-6363
http://www.esquinacarlosgardel.com.ar

This relatively new establishment is named after the tango icon Carlos Gardel who died prematurely in an airplane accident in 1935. It is located in the heart of the historic Abasto *barrio* where Gardel's mother lived.

The cobblestone street in front of this club bustles on the

weekend with locals and tourists. The Abasto mall is across the street on *Calle Anchorena*. A few doors away from Esquina Gardel are a number of sidewalk cafés, tango shoe stores and souvenir shops. (See Chapter 6: Shopping for Tango in BsAs). The one and a half hour show at this locale begins at 10:00 PM, with dinner served at 9:00 PM.

Cost in *pesos*: $$$

Esquina Homero Manzi
San Juan 3601 (Corner of Boedo; Bo. Boedo)
Tel: 4957-8488
http://www.esquinahomeromanzi.com.ar/

This "*bar notable*" is named after one of the most prolific tango composers, Homero Manzi. It dates back to 1927, but was totally renovated in 2000. There is also a tango written by Manzi about this corner, called "San Juan y Boedo." The restaurant is filled with pictures of some of the great tango protagonists. It is a large restaurant and is open for lunch during the day. There is also a nightly *cena-tango* show featuring live music, dancers, and singers. While the restaurant packs in visitors, many are Argentine. The show changes frequently and hosts guest artists.

Cost in *pesos*: $$

La Ventana
Balcarce 431 (Bo. San Telmo)
Tel: 4334-1314
http://www.la-ventana.com.ar

This dedicated theater hosts a nightly dinner show in the heart of the historic *barrio* of San Telmo. The cobblestone street on which it is located, Balcarce, has become a tourist center and features a number of other dinner clubs and theaters.

Cost in *pesos*: $$$

Madero Tango
Moreau de Justo (Corner of Brasil; Bo. Puerto Madero)
Tel: 5239-3009
http://www.maderotango.com
    This establishment is located in the heart of the upscale Puerto Madero waterfront section of BsAs. It is a spacious modern facility offering a nightly show with dinner served at 8:30 PM and show time at 10:00 PM.
Cost in *pesos*: $$

Michelangelo
Balcarce 433 (Bo. San Telmo)
Tel: 4342-7007
http://www.michelangelotango.com.ar
    This is an elegant dinner club in the heart of San Telmo. While it opened its renovated doors in 1967, the building itself dates back to 1849. The cobblestone street on which it is located has become a tourist center and features a number of other clubs. Michaelangelo begins serving it pre-fixe dinner around 8:30 PM at night.
Cost in *pesos*: $$$

Piazzolla Tango
Florida 165, Galería Guemes, lower level (Bo. Centro)
Tel: 4344-8201/02
http://www.piazzollatango.com
    This is a beautifully restored theater with its own art gallery. It is located on the lower level of the Galería Guemes, a shopping mall of independent stores on *Calle* Florida. While their show highlights the more avant-garde music of Piazzola, traditional tango pieces are also included.
Cost in *pesos*: $$$

Sabor a Tango
Gral JD Peron 2535 (Bo. Once)
Tel: 4953-8700
http://www.saboratango.com.ar
    This is a restored theater that dates back to 1878. Lunch is served daily. On Mondays through Sundays there is a *cena* show.
Cost in *pesos*: $$$

Señor Tango
Vieytes 1655 (Bo. Boca/ Barracas)
Tel: 4303 0231
http://www.senortango.com.ar
    This very spacious theater is located in the historical barrio of La Boca, the waterfront area where tango has its roots.
Cost in *pesos*: $$$

Taconeando
Balcarce 725 (Bo. San Telmo)
Tel: 4307-6696
http://www.taconeando.com//english/MENU_e.html
    This restaurant is in the heart of San Telmo in a relatively smaller space than other *cena* shows. The show is a recounting of the history of tango in music, song, and dance, combining traditional and modern elements.
Cost in *pesos*: $$

Tango Porteño
Cerrito 570 (Faces Av 9 de Julio; Bo. Centro)
Tel: 4124-9400
http://www.tangoporteno.com.ar
    This is a new addition to the *cena-tango* show circuit. It is a modern day recreation, art-deco style of an old theater and tango hall of the 1920s–1940s. The original hall was located around the corner on Av Corrientes. It is steps away from

the *Obelisco,* close to the intersection of Av 9 de Julio and Corrientes, in the heart of the theater district.

Cost in *pesos*: $$

Restaurant-Cafés with Shows

The previous section focused on theater-restaurants with a dedicated dinner-show. The restaurant-bars and cafés listed below offer a full menu and, on some nights, a scaled down show with a few musicians, possibly one or two singers. These shows are much less expensive and less spectacular. Generally, the restaurants are more intimate and also more authentic. This is tango for the locals and for music aficionados. Their shows may change nightly or weekly. Many of these places have been designated as "*Bares Notables*" by an act of government, because of their history, the fame of their patrons, their cultural value, and/or architectural design.

In this section, the restaurants, bars, and cafés are listed alphabetically, followed by short descriptions and, in some cases, prices in effect at the beginning of 2009. In Chapter 7, they are organized by *barrio*, enabling the reader to walk around the neighborhoods collecting flyers from the restaurants about their current shows. Alternatively, flyers are placed on their doors or glass fronts. Flyers are the most current and reliable sources of information on what these smaller establishments are currently offering. In addition, many have developed Web sites (included when available) that list the events of the month.

Bar Sur
Estados Unidos 299 (Corner of Balarce; Bo. San Telmo)
Tel: 4362-6086
http://www.bar-sur.com.ar

This is one of the "notable bars" dating back to the 1920s when it went under the name of Union Bar. Its current reincarnation opened in 1967. It is an intimate space with a great deal of character and history in the heart of San Telmo. Ongoing performances of singers and dancers start at 8:00 PM and continue till 2:00 AM.

Bien Porteño
Av. Rivadavia 1392 (Corner of Uruguay; Bo. Monserrat)
Tel: 4383-5426
http://www.bienporteno.com

This intimate restaurant and tango bar offers lunch daily, accompanied by recorded tango music and an open floor for dancing. On Mondays through Fridays there is a tango class after 4:00 PM, and on Friday and Saturday nights there is live entertainment. There is even a *milonga* on some afternoons and nights.

Café Montserrat
San Jose 524 (Bo. Monserrat)
Tel: 4381-2588
http://www.cafemontserrat.com

This is a charming, intimate bohemian café-bar with a changing art exhibit and live music, poetry readings, and other literary events. Up to four nights a week there is a show featuring folk, jazz, or tango musicians. On some nights there is an open mike. Starting time varies and on some nights there are two shows. A monthly calendar of performances is available at the café. Some events are free and for others there is a cover charge of up to 20 *pesos*. There is also a minimum consumption of 10 *pesos*. During the day, the café serves a light breakfast and lunch, as well as drinks.

Café Tortoni
Av. de Mayo 825 (Bo. Monserrat)
Tel: 4342-4328
http://www.cafetortoni.com.ar

This is one of the first bar-cafés in BsAs, dating back to
1858. At the turn of the twentieth
century it became a center for the
intellectual and artistic elite and is
named in a number of tangos,
including one entitled *Café Tortoni.*

The café still maintains its interior
elegance. There are two rooms that
offer shows seven nights a week,
Sala Alfonsina Storni and *La Bodega.*
Invited artists change frequently and
shows are usually advertised in the
local newspaper or on signs at the
entrance to this historic café (*bar notable*). Shows feature
live music, a singer, and a dance couple(s). Tickets can be
purchased in advance and currently run 60–70 *pesos*.

Clásica y Moderna
Av. Callao 892 (Bo. Norte)
Tel: 4812-8707
http://www.Clásicaymoderna.com

This intimate and lovely restaurant-bar/bookstore/art gallery
has nightly shows (Monday–Sunday) that change constantly.
At least one or two shows a week feature tango. Reservations
are recommended because the space is small and the locale is
popular. There is a cover charge for music depending on the
performer (from 20–40 *pesos*) and a minimum consumption is
expected of 15–25 *pesos*. The kitchen is open all day for lunch
and dinner. The restaurant advertises its monthly agenda on a
lovely postcard that is available at the beginning of the month,
as well as on the restaurant's Web site.

El Vesuvio Resto Cultural
Corrientes 1187 (Bo. Centro)
Tel: 4384-0986

http://www.restoelvesuvio.com.ar

This is a new addition to Av Corrientes, an intimate and elegant restaurant open for lunch and dinner. Tango shows are offered Fridays and Saturdays after 10:00 PM as an accompaniment to the restaurant's a la carte dinner.

Esquina Osvaldo Pugliese
Boeda 909 (Corner of Carlos Calvo; Bo. Boedo)
Tel: 4931-2142

This is a small local restaurant with a full lunch and dinner menu. It is named after Pugliese, a prolific tango musician, writer, and orchestra leader. The walls of this restaurant are lined with a great deal of tango memorabilia. On some nights there is an open mike and on other nights a very inexpensive cena-tango show.

La Cumparsita
Chile 302 (Corner of Balcarce; Bo. San Telmo)
Tel: 4361-6880

This restaurant offers a daily show of singers, dancers, and live music with light fare. The show is ongoing and runs from 10:30 PM–4:00 AM for 120 *pesos*.

Los 36 Billares
Avenida de Mayo 1265 (Bo. Monserrat)
Tel: 4381-5696.

http://www.los36billares.com.ar

This bar-restaurant opened in 1894. It is one of the more traditional bars of Buenos Aires (*Bar notable*) and is open for breakfast, lunch, and dinner. In addition to the entertainment that is featured Friday and Saturday nights, billiards and pool can be played. There is a charge of 20 *pesos* for the show (*entrada*), with a minimum of 15 *pesos* for dinner and drinks. The show, consisting of a few musicians, dance couples, and singers, begins between 9:00 PM and 10:00 PM, depending on the night and how filled the restaurant is.

Restaurants with Recorded Music or Tango History

The restaurants included in this section offer a full menu. Most are open for lunch, but close their doors for a few hours before beginning to serve dinner around 9:00 PM.

These restaurants are connected to tango in a variety of ways. Some may play tango as background music, while others simply have pictures or murals of tango protagonists on their walls. Still others have a great deal of history and have been the subject of tangos. A few have Web sites that are worth visiting, since they usually provide historical information about the restaurant, its connection to tango, and pictures of the restorations that they have undergone.

Café de Los Angelitos
Rivadavia 2100 (Bo. Balvanera/Congreso)
Tel: 4952-2320
http://www.cafedelosangelitos.com

The original café dates back to the 1890s. The new structure recently opened its doors as a restaurant by day and a *cena* show by night (See section in this chapter on dinner-shows). The walls include pictures of the original café and protagonists of the tango genre. The restaurant is opened all day. A guitarist and/or a *bandoneónista* play tango softly from a small balcony inside the restaurant Tuesdays–Sundays between 2:00 PM and 3:00 PM, and 7:00 PM and 8:00 PM.

Chiquilín
Sarmiento 1599 (Corner of Montevideo; Bo. Centro)
Tel: 4374-5163
http://www.chiquilín-argentina.com.ar

This full-scale restaurant is featured in a beautiful tango, Chiquilín de Batin, written by Horacio Ferrer. It is a very well kept restaurant that dates back to 1927. It is open seven days a week for lunch and dinner. The restaurant has been designated as a historical landmark.

Confitería Las Violetas
Rivadavia 3899 (Bo. Almagro)
http://www.lasvioletas-cafe.com.ar

This is a beautifully renovated historical building, surrounded by French stained glass windows and curved glass doors. It dates back to 1920 and has been awarded historical status. The restaurant serves breakfast, lunch, and dinner, but is noted for its pastries. The connection to tango is the lyricist Contursi, who frequented Las Violetas.

El Vesuvio Confitería / Heladería
Corrientes 1181 (Bo. Centro)
Tel: 4382-3735

This is an ice cream parlor/café that offers a full lunch and dinner menu. It has a strong tango history dating back to 1902. Tango greats that visited this establishment are featured on its walls. On Mondays, it offers a free tango music show, usually beginning after 10:00 PM. Start-up time should be verified.

La Esquina de Anibal Troilo
Paraguay 1500 (Corner of Parana; Bo. Norte)
Tel: 4811-6352

This restaurant features a gallery of over three hundred photos covering over fifty years of tango history. It is where Anibal Troilo, orchestra leader and *bandeonista*, would meet with friends and musicians. It has been given historical landmark status for its tango history.

Lalo's
Montevideo 353 (Bo. Centro)

This restaurant is decorated with tango photos and artwork. It is visited by some of the tango greats such as Horacio Ferrer, the poet and author, and Miguel Angel Zotto, the famous tango dancer. The food here is good, especially this restaurant's flambéed apple crepes (*panqueques de manzana con ron*). A pianist plays tangos (and other tunes) on request on Wednesdays after 10:00 PM and Saturdays after midnight.

Los Inmortales
Calle Corrientes 1369 (Bo. Centro)
Calle LaValle 746 (Near Calle Florida; Bo. Centro)
Calle Parana 1209 (Bo. Norte)
http://www.losinmortales.net

All three of these branches of Los Inmortales have papered their walls with old photos and photo collages of the tango greats. They offer a full menu, including pizza, pasta, salad, meats, and chicken.

Pan y Arte Resto Bar
Boedo 880 (Bo. Boedo)
Tel: 4957-6702

This restaurant and outdoor café has a limited but interesting organic menu, serving breakfast and lunch from 8:00 AM–4:00 PM, and dinner between 9:00 PM and 11:00 PM. It sometimes offers live tango music or plays recorded music. It also displays art. On a Saturday afternoon I sat in the outdoor café listening to the strains of tango by Piazzolla.

Parrilla Bravo
Matheu 24 (off Rivadavia, 2400 block; Bo. Balvanera)
Tel: 4953-2040

This restaurant is small and specializes in grilled meats (*parrilla al carbon)* and homemade dishes (*comidas caseras)*. The walls are decorated with a great deal of tango memorabilia, including posters, art, pictures and newspaper clippings. The owner, Omar Escudero, was a tango singer with Donato Racciati. Recorded tango music is played softly in the background. Omar will sometimes sing on request for guests/friends.

Pepito's
Montevideo 383 (Bo. Centro)
Tel. 4374-4514.

This restaurant, a few doors away from Lalo's Restaurant, is closer to *Calle* Corrientes. It too features artwork with a tango theme. Lunch and dinner are served.

FOOD CHOICES IN BUENOS AIRES

BsAs is a meat, potato, and pasta city. Portions are generally large, especially portions of beef. While there are many restaurants that are open all day, and late into the night for breakfast, lunch, and dinner, others close after lunch at around 3:00 PM. This is especially true in the case of *parrillas* that grill meat to order. They generally re-open around 8:30 PM or 9:00 PM, when they begin serving dinner. This timetable is also true for buffets (*tenedor libre*). These same restaurants usually stay open until after midnight. Throughout the city and generally near *milongas*, you will find some restaurants that remain open until the wee hours of the morning, even if it is just a pizzeria. This is especially the case in the downtown area referred to as El Centro.

While feeding my tango frenzy in BsAs, I tried to avoid heavy meals before dancing. For me, there is nothing worse than dancing on a heavy stomach, except not dancing at all. Therefore, lunch eaten late or dinner eaten early is often my big meal. I look for a few favorite restaurants near my residence that are open all day so that I can eat at a time that makes sense for my dancing and digesting timetable. Often when going to an early evening *milonga*, I eat a light dinner after dancing. If

I arrive hungry at a *milonga*, I order a thin-pressed sandwich (*tostada*) and a beverage.

Some of the foods, in translation, that go into a typical meal in BsAs:

- **Breakfast** (*desayuno*) tends to be light, consisting of:
  - coffee (*café*)
  - *medialunas* (croissants) made of butter *(de manteca)* or lard (*de grasa*)
  - sandwiches (*tostados*; toasted white bread, pressed thin, made of ham and/or cheese; untoasted versions are called *migas*)
  - freshly squeezed juice *(exprimido)*
  - fruit shakes *(liquados)* made either with milk (*con leche*) or with water (*con agua*)

- **Lunch** (*almuerzo*) is heavier, especially since dinner is eaten much later (after 9:00 PM). For many, lunch is a full meal with meat (*carne*) or fish (*pescado*), mashed potatoes (*puré de papas*), and fresh salad (*ensalada*). It begins around noon. Some restaurants stop serving around 3:00 PM. Lighter options, which dancers may prefer, include:
  - pizza in many forms
  - *empanadas* (ground meat, chicken, or ham and cheese wrapped in dough)
  - *choripán* (meat sausage (*chorizo*) opened and grilled, and served on bread (*pan*))

- **Dinner** (*cena/comida*) is served late and usually includes:
  - meat (*bife*), chicken (*pollo*), or fish (*pescado*) served with potatoes (*papas*)
  - pasta served with a variety of sauces (*salsas*)
  - salad (*ensalada*)

- dessert (*postre*)
- wine (*vino*)

Some popular Argentinean beverages and dishes you can order:

- **Beverages (*bebidas*)**
    - water (*aqua mineral*)
    carbonated (*con gas*)
    non-carbonated (*sin gas*)
    at room temperature (*natural*)
    - seltzer (*soda*)
    - carbonated soda (*gaseosa)*
    - grapefruit drink (*cuatro pomelos*)
    - freshly squeezed juice (*exprimido)* – made from fresh fruit, mostly oranges (*naranjas*), grapefruits (*pomelos*), lemons (*limones*)
    - beer (*cerveza*) – served in liters or small bottles
    - wines (*Vino*) – as inexpensive as soda, sometimes even cheaper. Argentina is noted for its malbec wine.
    - mixed drinks – expensive and not always prepared the way you may be accustomed to drinking them

- **Coffee (café)** is the preferred hot drink and is offered in a variety of ways, but generally with hot or steamed milk. Some coffee options are:
    - *lagrimita* – mostly steamed milk with some coffee
    - *café con leche* – half milk and half coffee
    - *café doble* – a double-sized order of *café con leche*
    - *cortado/cortadito* – espresso with some steamed milk

- *café Americano* – weaker coffee, generally
served with cold milk at the table

For a wonderful article about the coffee culture in BsAs and a description of a café, you must read the article attached to this link: http://aands.virginia.edu/x7076.xml.

• *Mate* is a local herbal tea usually drunk unsweetened from a gourd, and shared by sipping through a kind of straw (*bombilla*). It usually takes time to develop a taste for this national drink.

• **Beef dishes (*carne/bife*)** consist of cuts of steak generally grilled (*a la parilla*). They can be requested rare (*vuelta y vuelta* or *jugoso*), medium (*al punto*), or well done (*bien cocido*).
- *bife de Chorizo* – sirloin cut
- *asado* – rack of roasted short ribs
- *lomo* – filet mignon cut
- *choripán* – grilled open sausage (*chorizo*)
sandwich served on bread (*pan*)
- *estofado* – spaghetti sauce with chunks of
beef, akin to a beef stew
- *peceto* – pot roast, generally served with
roasted potatoes
- *milanesa* – breaded and fried veal cutlet

• **Chicken dishes (*pollo*)**
- *suprema* – breaded chicken cutlet
- *suprema de pollo napolitana* – breaded
chicken cutlet with ham, tomato sauce, and
mozzarella cheese
- *pata* – leg and thigh; dark meat
- *pechuga* – breast; white meat
- *deshuesado* – boneless
- *grille* - grilled
- *al horno* – baked

- frito - fried

• **Pork (*cerdo*)**

• **Fish (*pescado*)**

• **Potatoes (*papas*),** including sweet potatoes (*batatas*), can be served as fried (*frita*), mashed (*puré*), thinly sliced and fried chips (*españoles*), and sautéed round potato balls (*noisette*).

• **Salad (*ensalada*)** – generally you specify what you want in your salad and you pay according to the number of items you select. The most popular inclusions are lettuce (*lechuga*), tomatoes (*tomates*), carrots (*zanahorias*), beets (*remolachas*), onions (*cebollas*), peas (*arvejas*), olives (*aceitunas*), corn (maíz or *choclo*), etc.

• **Empanadas** are small crescent pies filled with meat (*carne*) (hot (*picante*) or mild (*suave*)), chicken (*pollo*), ham and cheese (*jamón y queso*), or with mozzarella (*caprese*), among other fillings. They can be baked (*al horno*) or fried (*frita*).

• **Pastas** are very popular and not usually served al dente. A great deal of pasta is made fresh (*pasta casera*) either on the premises or in a local pasta shop and it is often on the soft side. You can ask for it al dente, but don't expect a crunch.

• **Sauces (*salsa*)** for your pasta are almost always ordered separately. Some common sauces include tomato sauce (*tuco or fileto*), meat sauce (*bolognesa*), chunks of beef in sauce (*estofado*), or cream sauce made with four cheeses (*cuatro quesos*).

• **Desserts (*postres*)** – some of the most popular desserts include flan with cream (*crema*), or their famous *dulce de leche*, bread pudding (*pudín*), ice cream (*helado*), and my favorite, apple crepes flambéed with rum (*panqueques de manzana con ron*), a sweet meal unto itself.

A CLOSING NOTE

Argentina is a country noted for its beef, but I was rarely disappointed with any of the foods I ate. What I most enjoyed, however, was the attitude of the people towards meals. They are a social event, not to be rushed, but rather to be savored. Enjoy the food, the people, the pace, and the hospitality, and if you can do it with tango as a backdrop or up front and on stage, so much the better.

¡BUEN PROVECHO!

Chapter 3
Studying Tango

"El abrazo es más importante que el paso." (Gavito)
("The embrace is more important than the step.")

"El tango es un sentimiento que hay que incorporar en la danza." (*milonguero* anon)
("Tango is a sentiment that you must incorporate into your dance.")

Tango, like any other art form, is a dance that tango aficionados are always perfecting. Even after twelve years of dancing, I continue to learn more, not just about the dance, but also about movement and about my body. The placement of my feet and steps is incidental to the movement of my body, to my axis, and equilibrium. More importantly, I have learned the critical role of the connection to my partner and to the music. However, this shift of focus from steps to movement and from form to feeling took time to develop.

OVERVIEW

This chapter was written to provide a cursory introduction to some of the more popular teaching/learning venues and to the most established schools and teachers. The tango publications,

BA Tango, *Tangauta*, and *La Milonga* (introduced in Chapter 1) have comprehensive lists and advertisements of schools, studios, teachers, and classes offering tango instruction throughout BsAs. However, the choices are daunting and even intimidating, especially for the first-time visitor to this city. In this chapter you will find a short list of some of the places and people with whom I have studied and from whom many of my insights into tango came.

The chapter begins with an overview from my perspective and after years of studying and dancing tango, of the essential elements of the dance, emphasizing the connection to one's partner and to the music. The remainder of the chapter is divided into two sections. The first describes schools, studios, and dance halls where tango is taught and practiced, and what you can expect to find at each. The second section gives you the critical vocabulary needed to take full advantage of tango instruction, which in BsAs is often provided only in Spanish. Throughout the chapter, critical dance vocabulary is translated into Spanish to enable the reader to understand the language of the classroom.

BEYOND STEPS: ESSENTIAL ELEMENTS OF THE DANCE

When I first started to study tango, I would watch the advanced class wistfully. I couldn't wait to be in there with them. I dismissed the basics as trite and boring. While I knew that walking was important, I wanted to dance, and to me that meant being able to do lots of steps. In those days, my dance partners were also relatively new to the dance. They believed (as I did) that by focusing on the placement of our feet, we could master the dance.

I have come full circle. After years of dancing, I have returned to the basics. I continue to work on perfecting my dancing and my walking, but now I do so in terms of my connection to my partner, first and foremost. I focus on my axis, my extension, and my tension (or lack thereof), my ability to disconnect my upper torso from my lower torso, of keeping my knees soft and together, and of caressing the floor—all of this while maintaining that magical connection.

The feeling with which I dance comes from both my connection to my partner and to the music. And yes, I am still discovering what makes this dance so powerful, beautiful, and fulfilling. Now I listen to the music more frequently and intensively, and I respond differently to different orchestras, voices, and rhythms.

Every trip to Argentina has given me greater insight. I now know that even in silence and stillness there is movement and it needs to be fluid. However, movement is sometimes invisible to the spectator. Even in pauses, there is energy. Gavito, a famous *milonguero*, performer, and teacher, was described by one of his partners, Marcella, as a man who made pauses eternal (*hace las pauses eternas*). And yet, if you watch Gavito on YouTube, you can see clearly that his pauses have energy and even movement, albeit subtle. He marks time and responds to a beat or a musical phrase, even as he remains in one spot. It could be with a simple and slow shift or settling of weight (*cambio/traslado de peso*), or a subtle move of his torso, or a change in his embrace (*el abrazo*). For this, a woman must learn patience. She must wait, with energy also, until led to do something different, or to move someplace else.

I have also learned that the embrace frames the dance and is an integral part of it. It defines the space between partners. More importantly, *el abrazo* creates the connection that is at the heart of the dance. It establishes the inner communication that must go on between partners in order to dance harmoniously.

The problem is that too often we learn steps, sequences, and patterns at the expense of knowing how to move beautifully and elegantly to the music (*al compás*). For seasoned dancers in BsAs, the walk (*el caminar*) is what counts. Walking is the foundation of the dance. *Milongueros* often compare learning to walk in tango with learning to walk as a toddler; they equate learning steps to running. They say that people learning tango seem to want to run before they can walk.

Even after years of dancing, I still take group and private lessons. I even host practice sessions (*prácticas*) in my home. These classes and *prácticas* always bring me back to the basics: the walk and body movement, my axis, equilibrium, form, and my connection to my partner.

Even more basic is feeling (*el sentir*). A teacher once told me, "You know how to dance, now just listen and feel (*sentís*)." He talked about feeling my partner (in the figurative sense, of course), and about feeling the music. "Listen (*Escuchá*) to the music through my body." I now wear my partner like an old and close-fitting shirt. I never disconnect from him unless led to do so. And I *wait* for that lead *(la marcación).*

CONNECTION TO THE MUSIC

In turn, I never disconnect from the music. However, connection to the music means different things to different dancers, depending on the moment, the orchestra, and the lyrics, among other variables. Sometimes my partner is listening to the melody and at other times it is the rhythm (*el compás*) or an instrument that inspires him. It could be the *bandoneón* or the violin that is the driving force in his dancing, and in his interpreting the music to and with his partner.

I have had the opportunity over many trips to observe and get to know many *milongueros.* Each one has a way of viewing the dance and of interpreting it. One *milonguero* told me that in order to dance tango you need balance, an ear for the music, and posture. (*Para bailar tango se necesita equilibrio, armonía, y postura*). Other *milongueros* focus exclusively on the music (*cadencia y compás*). It is evident in how and when they step to the music and how they mark time when they are in a holding pattern on a crowded dance floor. As noted earlier, they can step on the beat, move through it, or pause on it. One move can be stretched over three or four beats. To me, that slower cadence is the beauty of the dance and what possesses me to want to dance with certain individuals. Truth be said, it is what drives me crazy about the dance.

All of these variables are, I feel, at the heart of what makes tango both beautiful and challenging.

THE SELECTION AND ROLE OF TEACHERS

What I have learned through classes is that there are many ways of moving and not all teachers (*maestros*) are in agreement about the essence of that movement. In fact one teacher might emphasize a soft body frame, while another will stress some resistance. The challenge is to draw from all your sources, and develop your own style, i.e. what seems to fit and resonate with you.

For me, every teacher has something to offer. In reality, however, not all teachers are good at communicating, much less teaching, even if they are excellent dancers. I have found this to be the case with some well-known *milongueros*. Keep in mind that sometimes we gain more by observing, rather than by listening and following directions. Therefore, as a student, you must learn to listen with your eyes and to dance with your heart.

When classes are taken, you want them to be rewarding, constructive, and in the long run, to move your dance to another level. You are in BsAs to make your dancing the most pleasurable experience, both for you and your partner. You are also there to feel good about your dancing and to look good to the onlooker, so that you get asked to dance more often. To that end, guided instruction and professional feedback serve an important purpose. But so does careful observation of the best *milongueros* dancing socially. (See Chapter 4: *Milongueando* in BsAs for a list of *milongas* that attract seasoned *milongueros*.)

TANGO CLASSES

Schools and Studios

In BsAs, there are many schools (*escuelas*) of tango and dance studios (*estudios*) that offer a comprehensive array of group classes throughout the day for up to six days a week. They also offer you the opportunity to take classes with a variety of teachers, so that you settle with the one that supports you most comfortably while moving your dancing to another level. Rates for group classes are very reasonable (from 15 to 30 *pesos*). Sometimes discounts are available when packages of classes are purchased. Many schools also offer the option of private classes with your instructor. This is a sampling of some of the more popular schools/studios that offer classes in tango, *milonga*, and waltz (*tango vals).*

• Estudio DNI Tango
Av Corrientes 2140 (Bo. Balvanera/Once)
Calle Bulnes 1011/13 (Bo. Almagro)
Tel: 4866-3663
http://www.dni-tango.com

Getting to Corrientes: *Subte* Line B to *Pasteur* station (on Av Corrientes). Walk two blocks on Corrientes to DNI
Getting to Bulnes: Subte Line B to Medrano station (on Av Corrientes). It is a short walk away from Corrientes to the studio.

   DNI is run by Pablo Villarraza and Dana Frígoli, with the support of a team of teachers. Both Pablo and Dana are well known throughout Argentina, Europe, and Canada. At their studio, they offer an array of classes for tango, *milonga*, and *vals* from Monday to Saturday, starting at 11:30 AM until 8:30

PM. Classes are organized by level, from 1–6. The studio is very popular with the international set. On Saturday afternoons there is a *práctica* open to all students. DNI also offers classes in yoga, contemporary dance, and women's technique (*técnica para mujeres*). Check out their Web site for a complete listing of classes.

The teachers at this school share a philosophy about tango and an approach to teaching that I found extremely useful. Their focus is on body movement and energy in dancing. They are also involved with the social tango scene and know where to go to see both young people and older *milongueros* dancing.

Spanish is the dominant language used for instruction, with a sprinkling of English. However, there is often someone in class who is fully bilingual and who will translate when the teacher gets stuck trying to explain a subtlety of the dance or the energy behind a movement.

DNI studios exude a wonderful community feeling. Both townhouses include a reception area, a boutique, a kitchen, and studios used for group instruction and private classes. Space can also be rented for practice.

• Escuela Argentina de Tango (EAT)
Calle Viamonte (Corner of San Martín; Bo. Centro)
Tel: 4312-4990
http://www.eatango.org

Getting there: *Subte* Line C, Lavalle station; a three-block walk to *Calle* Florida and Viamonte

The school, EAT, is housed in the *Centro Cultural (CC) Borges* that is located inside *Galerías Pacífico*, a beautiful upscale mall. The mall's main entrance is on *Calle* Florida. The cultural center is around the back of the mall and on the second level. It is more easily accessible behind the mall, on *Calle Viamonte*, corner of *San Martín*. However, you can also access it through the mall. (While you are at the *Galería* don't forget to pick up a small folding map of the city (*plano turístico*)).

EAT offers classes seven days a week, from 9:30 in the morning until 10:00 at night in ninety-minute blocks. The last set of classes begins at 8:30 PM. There are classes in tango, waltz (*vals*), *milonga, milonga con traspie, canyengue*, women's technique (*técnica para la mujer*), and complex figures in close embrace (*figuras complejas en abrazo cerrado*), among others.

The school has an excellent and extensive core of teachers (*maestros*), and classes are sometimes small. However, with the more popular teachers (e.g., Aurora Lubiz, Gachi Fernandez, Jorge Firpo, Jorge Torres, Esther and Mingo Pugliese, Dany el Flaco, the Riverolas) classes are generally full. Among the lesser-known teachers, I have found some excellent instruction, and with small classes I have enjoyed superb feedback. What is important is finding a teacher with whom you resonate. I always looked for someone who was able to spot a problem easily or to break down movements into digestible units.

EAT puts out a monthly flyer indicating the classes and special seminars that are scheduled for the month. All classes appear with either a P, I, or A on the right corner, indicating whether the class is for beginning (*principiantes*), intermediate (*intermedios*), or advanced (*avanzados*) students. If you find the right teacher(s), you can arrange for private lessons with them.

While most of the teaching takes place at the *Galería* (*Sede Centro*), some classes are offered at their satellite *(sede)* in *Bo. Norte - Sede Talcahuano* at Talcahuano 1052.

Their Web site is quite complete. Each month they list every course and teacher, as well as special seminars being offered at their both locations.

• Nuevo Estudio La Esquina
Sarmiento 722, 4th floor (*piso* 4) (Bo. Centro)
Tel: 4394-9898

Getting there: *Subte* Line B to *Carlos Pellegrini*, or Line C to *Diagonal Norte*, or Line D to *9 de Julio*
Classes are offered from 10:00 AM to 10:00 PM daily by a variety of teachers. The studio also offers special seminars focused on specific techniques such as displacements, *boleos*, *colgadas*, embellishments, and musicality. Studio space is also available for rent.

• National Academy of Tango (*Academia Nacional del Tango*) (entrance is next to Café Tortoni)
Av. de Mayo 833, 1st floor, i.e. one flight up (Bo. Monserrat)
Tel: 4345-6967/Telefax: 4345-6968

Getting there: *Subte* Line A to *Piedras*
Tango classes are offered Monday to Friday evenings from 3:00 PM till 9:00 PM. In addition, there is a tango museum housed on another floor of the same building. The museum is described in detail in Chapter 5.

• Tango-Escuela Carlos Copello
Anchorena 575 (Bo. Abasto)
Tel: 4864-6229
http://www.carloscopello.com

Getting there: *Subte* Line B to *Gardel* station. The school is located across the street from the Abasto Shopping Center.
This studio is a comprehensive dance studio in Bo. Abasto. It is open seven days a week from early afternoon till 9:00 PM. Classes are offered in tango as well as folklore, rock and roll, swing, salsa, arabe, and hip-hop. Tango classes feature some

well-known dancers. Their Web site highlights the teachers and lists the classes. A monthly schedule of classes is available, as is studio space for rent.

The *barrio* of Abasto has a strong tango history, including a museum of Gardel (Chapter 5) and good shopping opportunities for tango shoes, clothing, and souvenirs (Chapter 6) on *Calle* Anchorena.

• Mora Godoy Tango Escuela
Av Pueyrredón 1090, 2ⁿᵈ floor *(piso 2)* **(Bo. Norte)**
Tel: 4964-0254 or 4966-1225
http://www.moragodoy.com

Getting there: *Subte* Line D to *Pueyrredón* station. There is a four-block walk to the studio.

This school offers three classes per day from Monday to Friday, one in the afternoon and two in the evening, taught by different teachers and focusing on different levels.

Practicás

Practice sessions (*prácticas*) give dancers an opportunity to practice with guidance and/or feedback. There are many listed in the tango guides, *BA Tango, Tangauta,* and *La Milonga.* The schools of tango listed above offer some. However, the practica that I found most helpful was:

• Confitería La Ideal
Suipacha 384, one flight up *(primer piso)*
Tuesdays and Fridays from 12:00 PM–3:00 PM
http://www.elabrazotango.com

Getting there: *Subte* Line C to *Diagonal Norte,* Line B to *Carlos Pellegrini*, or Line D to *9 de Julio*

The teachers Diego and Zoraida run the *abrazo* tango club as an informal class that includes personalized feedback as well as small group instruction, as deemed necessary by the teachers or as requested. They encourage students and visitors, both men and women, to ask anyone to dance. Participants are also encouraged to ask questions and seek guidance from them, but especially to dance. You get tourists for sure, but you also get to dance with some wonderful old timers. Be aware that some of the Argentines are there to meet a possible candidate for private lessons. This is the one place where women are allowed and even encouraged to ask men to dance. Diego and Zoraida do not want to see people sitting. The teachers/tutors are really wonderful in helping you work on what you want to improve. The Friday *practica* is followed by a popular afternoon *milonga* from 2:00 PM–8:30 PM.

Pre-*Milonga* Classes

Some *milongas* offer classes before their official *milonga* begins. Since these classes are inexpensive or even free when a ticket is purchased for the *milonga*, many foreigners and *porteños* take advantage of the bargain. Pre-*milonga* classes also give you the opportunity to be seen and to dance with others who are there for the lesson. Generally, lessons are conducted in Spanish. This is a great way to meet people, dance, be seen, and line up partners for the actual *milonga* that follows. More details about the clubs listed below can be found in Chapter 4: *Milongueando* in BsAs.

1) **La Ideal** (Suipacha 384, near Av Corrientes; Bo. Centro).
    A class precedes many afternoon and late night *milongas* at this establishment. Classes are offered at different times, from Monday to Sunday. It is best to pick up their folded monthly agenda and/or the individual flyers for *milongas* and classes available on the ground floor. This is something that should

be done as soon as you arrive in Buenos Aires.

2) **El Beso** (Riobamba 416, near Av Corrientes; Bo. Centro)
This club gives *milonguero*-style tango classes on Mondays, Wednesdays, Fridays, Saturdays, and Sundays, beginning around 8:00 PM or 8:30 PM before their popular late night *milonga*. One of the teachers, Maria Plazaola, was Carlos Gavito's partner before he died. In addition, they have recently added early classes (at around 1:00 PM) from Monday to Friday focused also on *milonguero*-style dancing.

3) **Porteño and Bailarín** (Riobamba 345, near Av Corrientes; Bo. Centro)
This club offers classes Tuesday and Sunday nights beginning at around 9:00 PM, before their late night *milonga*. Well-known dancers, such as Ana Maria Schapira and the couple Ernesto Balmaceda and Stella Baez, often teach classes. Look up P*orteño* and *Bailarín* on YouTube to get a sense of the teachers that have performed there and the patrons that frequent the club.

4) **Salón Canning** (Scalabrini Ortiz 1331, near Av Córdoba; Bo Palermo Viejo)
This club offers classes on Wednesdays from 2:00 PM–4:00 PM before its popular early *milonga*. Night classes are also offered starting around 9:00 PM before their late *milongas* on Tuesday, Thursday, Friday, and Saturday.

Classes are given by well-known *milongueros* such as Jorge Firpo and Ana Maria Schipira. There is a good mix of ages at their *milongas* and in their classes.

5) **La Viruta** (Armenia 1366; Bo. Palermo Viejo) (http://lavirutatango.com/)
This club sponsors a popular *milonga* attracting a younger clientele interested in newer tango. They offer classes from Tuesday to Sunday, with an emphasis on figures and *nuevo tango*.

6) **Niño Bien** (Humberto Primo 1462; Bo. Constitución)
This club offers classes from 9:00 PM–10:30 PM before its popular Thursday night *milonga*.

7) **Torquatto Tasso** (Defensa 1575; Bo. San Telmo) (www.torquatotasso.com.ar).
Classes are offered Mondays through Sundays, and some are followed by a *milonga*.

8) **Club Gricel** (La Rioja 1180; Bo. Almagro)
Generally on Monday, Tuesday, Wednesday, Friday, Saturday, and Sunday, there is a class before this club's popular *milonga*. Start-up times and teachers vary by night.

9) **La Baldosa** (R.L. Falcón 2750)
Although off the beaten track, this Friday night *milonga* is very popular with all ages, usually because of the dancers that are

invited to perform. There is a class before the *milonga*, beginning around 8:30 PM.

Popular Teachers

The number of teachers that advertise and/or are listed in the tango magazines as providing group and/or private instruction is daunting.

The questions of whom to study with or what works for an individual are personal. I can only share my experience and recommend teachers and schools that have worked for me or for friends of mine who have visited BsAs often. While there are many teachers with whom I have studied and whom I can personally recommend, there are many more I have never met and who, I am sure work for others.

In selecting a teacher for private instruction, it is helpful to see them dance. At a minimum, their dancing needs to resonate with you. Obviously, you can see them dance by taking a group class with them. That also would give you an opportunity to see them teach. However, if your stay in BsAs is limited to a week or two, you may want to decide on a teacher even before you leave home. To that end, you can search on http://www.youtube.com by the name of the dancer/teacher. You can also search by *milonga* (e.g., "tango at *Porteño y Bailarín*" or by inserting any other club that was listed in the aforementioned section of "Pre-*milonga* classes").

Below (Table 2) is an alphabetical list of a few very popular teachers with whom I have studied or whose names kept surfacing as I sought out references from friends who have visited or who live in BsAs. Be aware that teachers who are well traveled and who have taught abroad may quote you a price in the currency of your home country. Therefore, it is always wise to verify that the price quoted is in *pesos*, rather than dollars.

TABLE 2

Dancers/Teachers	
WOMEN	**MEN**
Fernandez, Gachi	Cristaldo, Angel elangeldetango@arnet.com.ar (e-mail)
Godoy, Mora http://www.moragodoy.com	Firpo, Jorge jorgefirpo@sion.com (e-mail)
Gonzalez, Graciela tango@gracielagonzalez.com	Lapadula, Daniel http://www.inscenes.com/daniel. shtml?daniel
Lubiz, Aurora (Teaches at EAT, CC Borges)	**COUPLES**
Miller, Susana http://www.susanamiller. com.ar	Sebastian Achaval and Roxana Suarez http://roxanaysebastian.blogspot. com/
Plazaola, Maria (Teaches at El Beso)	Ernesto Balmaceda and Stella Baez http://ernestoystella.blogspot. com/
Plebs, Milena Milenaplebs.com	Julio Balmaceda and Corina de la Rosa http://julioycorina.com.ar/
Schapira, Ana Maria http://www.anaschapira. com.ar	Gustavo Benzecry Saba and Maria Olivera http://www.tangosalon.com.ar/
Rojas, Geraldine	Gustavo Naveira and Giselle Anne http://gustavoygiselle.com/

Poberaj, Natacha (Teaches at Copello's Academy)	Maria and Carlos Riverola (Teach at EAT, CC Borges)
	Pablo Villarraza and Dana Frígoli http://www.pabloydanatango.com.ar/agenda.html

Graciela Gonzalez periodically offers a popular and intensive four-hour tango workshop. The focus of the woman's workshop is on technique, and for the men the focus is on leading.

Private Classes with *Milongueros*

If you have a dance partner and want to practice privately, there are studios available that rent rooms by the hour. They are either listed or advertise in the monthly tango publications, *BA Tango, El Tangauta,* and *La Milonga.*

However, if you don't have a partner, there are acceptable ways of eliciting the paid help of *milongueros* in your quest for feedback and concentrated practice, especially in this economy. If I have seen or danced with someone that has impressed me, I have asked if they give lessons. Sometimes a man will offer his services by way of giving you some feedback on the dance floor. While it is impolite on his part, it nevertheless has served my interest.

Another alternative is to enlist the help of an agency or service that offers you "taxi dancers," *milongueros* who may teach and also accompany you to a *milonga*. It is not something I have tried, but it may serve those who are timid. Two Web sites that provide more information are: http://www.tangoargentinopartners.com/english.html and http://www.tangotaxidancers.com/InglesIntro.html.

In addition, if you make arrangements with a *milonguero* or a bona fide teacher, they usually find the space to practice.

If you rent a studio you need to find out if they have music. Generally, it is wise to bring your own CDs or to check with your instructor to be sure he/she brings music to which you want to practice. Studios usually have CD players, but check for their availability at the time you need it. For those who are video camera savvy, it is a good idea to tape yourself dancing with the teacher, obviously with his/her permission. I generally ask my teacher if I can tape the last ten minutes where we review what was covered. I have found that looking at the tape at my leisure was probably the best investment of time I made.

CRITICAL VOCABULARY
(*palabras claves*)
Needed for the Study of Tango

Many of the teachers in Buenos Aires speak only Spanish when teaching. If they have traveled a great deal, they probably know some other language or languages, enough to use pivotal words that will help you follow the class. However, a great deal is lost in translation, especially when they are trying to help you understand the reason for moving a certain way. As I took classes, I would note some of the critical terminology and dance principles that kept repeating themselves. To that end, the charts below were created. They provide translations of critical vocabulary that focuses on important dance principles, key body parts, tango moves, directionality, and encouragement.

1. Important Dance Principles

English	Spanish
Maintain your axis	*Mantener el eje*
Stretch the spinal column	*Estirar la columna (vertebral)*
Maintain (hold in) your belly button and tummy	*Mantener el umbligo y panza para dentro*
Extend your leg/torso	*Extender/ estirar la pierna/el torso*
Relax the shoulders/knees	*Relajar los hombros/las rodillas*
Separate your torso from your hip	*Separar el torso de la cadera*
Turn your hip in (out)	*Girar la cadera hacia delante (detrás)*
Keep your body soft	*Ponte blandita*
Step and move with the big toe (In moving it should be your first point of contact with the floor)	*Pisar con el dedo gordo*
Follow the man's shoulders	*Seguir los hombros del hombre*
Follow the line of dance	*Seguir la línea de la pista*
Step lightly	*Pisar suave*
Walk to the beat	*Caminar al compás*
Caress (maintain contact with) the floor	*Acariciar (mantener contacto con) el piso*
Maintain contact with the man's chest	*Mantener contacto con el pecho del hombre*
Tango consists of tension between movement and pauses	*Tango consiste en una tension entre movimiento y pausas*
Shift/change weight	*Trasladar/cambiar/pasar el peso*
Step into the space created by your partner moving	*Ocupar el lugar*

2. Key Body Parts

English	Spanish
Arm	*Brazo*
Elbow	*Codo*
Wrist	*Muñeca*
Joints	*Articulaciones*
Shoulder	*Hombro*
Chest	*Pecho*
Torso	*Torso*
Stomach	*Panza/barriga/estómago*
Hip	*Cadera*
Leg	*Pierna*
Foot	*Pie*
The big toe	*El dedo gordo*
Ankle	*Tobillo*
Front (of the foot)	*Punta del pie*
Heel of the foot/shoe	*Taco del pie/ zapato*

3. Tango Moves (*Movimiento*)

English	Spanish
To lead	*Marcar*
To get out of a move	*Salir de un paso*
Step lightly	*Pisar liviano*
Step heavily	*Pisar duro/fuerte*
To lean	*Apoyar*
To walk	*Caminar*
To cross	*Cruzar*

English	Spanish
To turn	*Girar*
To pivot	*Pivotear*
To walk around (encircle) the man/woman	*Rodear al hombre/mujer*
To extend	*Extender/estirar*
To open (the hip; shoulder)	*Abrir (la cadera; hombro)*
To close (the hip)	*Cerrar la cadera*
The embrace	*El abrazo*
The lead	*La marcación*
Displacement	*Sacada*
To displace	*Desplegar*
A step	*Un paso*
Short step	*Paso corto*
Long step	*Paso largo*
A side step	*Un paso al lado*
The walk	*El caminar*
A turn	*Un giro*
Bring the woman with you	*Traer la mujer*
Dance with cadence	*Bailar con cadencia*
Step to the beat	*Bailar al compás; llevar el compás*

4. Directionality

English	Spanish
To the right; to the left	*Al lado derecho; al lado izquierdo*
In front	*Al frente*
In back of; behind	*Detras; para tras.*

There	*Allí*
Here	*Aquí; Acá*

5. Encouragement

!Eso! – A spontaneous form of praise that Argentineans use to show their enthusiasm and approval. That is like getting an A+.

A CLOSING NOTE

There are two big lessons that I took away from my private and group classes. The first is that no one person has the ultimate secret. There are many secrets, many ways to personalize this dance, many ways to move, to mark time, and to respond to a partner. In essence, there are many ways to dance tango. That is in fact the ultimate beauty and challenge of the dance.

The second secret is that while lessons serve a purpose, they may also inhibit your dancing. Sometimes I have walked away from a lesson feeling incompetent and frustrated. The ultimate test is always the dance floor (*en la pista*), and that is where you really learn to dance. Automaticity in walking, moving without thinking, listening to my partner's body, and really hearing the music are my ultimate goals. And so, while lessons have their place in this very intricate and intimate dance, dancing truly is the ultimate test.

You need to take time to integrate what you have learned into your dancing. It is better to take one or two really important pieces of advice and work on that, rather than on trying to memorize a series of moves after each class.

Learning never is a linear activity, i.e., one does not learn and automatically use, remember, or improve one's dance after a lesson. Sometimes one step forward results in two steps backwards. Truly patience and practice (*en la pista*) will be your best friends.

Savor the journey!

Chapter 4
Milongueando in Buenos Aires
(The Tango Dance Scene)

"Así se baila el tango—cerrando los ojos para oir mejor."
("That is how you dance tango—closing your eyes to hear better.")

Lyrics to "Así Se Baila el Tango"

I am sitting at a table at one of my favorite clubs, El *Chiqué*, where this vacation began a week ago. The day I arrived was a euphoric experience. My first dance set was with a gentleman I had met on my previous trip; one whose dancing evoked my favorite expression, "Oh my God, I just died and went to heaven." That first *milonga* was spent renewing old friendships and dancing nonstop.

A week later I return. This time the experience is quieter. I want to bottle up this night, the music, the dancers, the feeling, and even the lighting. I observe

> well-dressed women with decorative fans sitting out a dance set (*tanda*), old and young *milongueros/as* dancing with partners of all ages and sizes. They dance with feeling and cadence (*con sentimiento y al compás*). They close their eyes, and wear the music on their faces. Some patrons are oblivious to the fact that this music is really about expressing a sentiment, and then there are those who know full well.

> Personal BA Journal,
> November 2008

You are in BsAs; most of you are there to dance until you can't bear it any longer. On my first trip I took classes in the afternoons, and danced in the evenings, and late into the wee hours of the morning. By the time I returned to my hotel, I had to ice my feet to be ready for the next marathon, later that day.

For me, dancing in BsAs is unlike dancing back home (New York), or for that matter unlike dancing in any other part of the world where I have danced. Many of my friends return to BsAs as often as possible. They do so because of the quality of the dancing, and the connection they are made to feel with their partners and with the music.

OVERVIEW

In order to fully immerse yourself in the culture of tango, a dancer (man or woman) should understand what differentiates a *milonguero* from other dancers. To that end, this chapter begins with a portrait of a *milonguero*. It describes men who were raised and groomed on tango and whose reverence for the dance and its traditions color their dancing.

The rest of this chapter focuses on the norms of behavior at a *milonga*. It covers what to do (and what not to do) and what to expect at a *milonga*. It ends with a review of the most popular spots for dancing.

The chapter is divided into four sections. The first is an overview of the tango scene in BsAs. This is followed by a description of the major monthly tango publications that give the most current information about tango in and around BsAs. The third section focuses on the clubs, including general information, appropriate behavior at *milongas*, and dance floor etiquette. The last section lists and briefly describes the most popular early and nighttime *milongas*. Addendum 2 offers the reader a weekly calendar and timetable for the recommended *milongas*. In this way readers can see at a glance the *milongas* that are available each day of the week.

PORTRAIT OF A *MILONGUERO*

El Abrazo
Pedro & Graciela: Photographer, Jan LaSalle

Throughout this book reference is made to "old *milongueros*," as a way of differentiating them from the younger generation of dancers who have taken a serious interest in the dance, but who do not have the history that the older dancers have. Old *milongueros* are men who were nursed on tango. They learned the dance at an early age and they ate, breathed, and listened to the music constantly. They know both the music and the lyrics. They feel it in their blood. Younger female dancers seek them out, "older" men who are just beginning or reviving their connection to tango respect them, and tourists admire them.

I use the term "old *milonguero*" with respect, albeit with some reservation. Generally speaking being called a *Milonguero* is a badge of honor, one that is bestowed on the dancer, rather than self-assigned. It neither signals an age, nor describes a performer. The term represents someone with a particular attitude towards the dance and the self. Old *milongueros* dress the part, respect the traditions, and dance non-pretentiously. They have a long-standing history with the dance. They live by the truism: *"El tango es un sentimiento triste que se baila"* ("Tango is a sad feeling/emotion to which one dances").

Milongueros often wear a jacket, if not a suit and tie. They do not converse during the dance, and they escort their partners off the dance floor. They know the floor (*pista*) like the palm of their hands. They do not bump into other dancers. They stay within their dancing space, often negotiating crowded dance floors with small, circular moves. You know you are among old *milongueros* by the cadence of the floor. Their movement is like the rise and fall of a gentle wave caressing the shore.

I am always moved by the *milonguero* who signals me to dance with a nonchalant nod of his head from across a crowded room, approaches my table buttoning his jacket, waits for the music to begin before negotiating the embrace, and releases the embrace after the music ends. I was once told by a wonderful *milonguero* that he decides when to end the dance.

Therefore, the dance does not always end with the music. For the *milonguero*, it ends when he releases the embrace.

Milongueros know that their role in the dance is to guide, lead, and protect the woman. It is never to show off what he knows and can do at the woman's expense. It is his role to make his partner look good. For if she looks good then he will look good.

Argentine men, *milongueros* notwithstanding, have a predilection for young and beautiful women, especially blondes. Some prefer dancing with Argentine women, while others prefer tourists because they have studied the dance and may follow easily. Still others may see in the outsider an opportunity to "teach." **Beware of the *milonguero* who tries to soft sell his services. Remember that a good dancer does not always make for a good teacher.** That being said, I once asked a wonderful dancer if he would be willing to practice with me. I am happy to say that it was a good experience, but that is not always the case. It is best that private teachers or practice partners be recommended by someone you trust.

Generally, *milongueros* are demanding (*exigente*) and selective in choosing a partner (*pareja*). They want to be seen with beautiful dancers in order to impress both their peers and strangers. They always want to look good on the dance floor (*pista*) since it is their ticket to even more women seeking them out as partners, albeit subtly—very subtly.

Milongueros also have musical preferences. They have favorite tangos, orchestras, and singers. Some only dance to specific orchestras and never others. By and large, *milongueros* do not dance to the music of Piazolla, or to tangos sung by Gardel. Some do not even like to dance to Pugliese's music. Others revel in Pugliese, with the tempo changes that characterize it. Many *milongueros* prefer the marked cadence of D'Arienzo, or the slower orchestrated tangos of DiSarli, or the older rhythms of Francisco Lomuto. While some *milongueros* are inspired by tangos with lyrics, others have told me that lyrics distract them while they are dancing. Some will sit out sets and listen with respect and melancholy, but will not dance. Clearly, not all tangos are a reason for dancing.

As a woman, exposed to many forms of tango music over the years, I learned to love the slow, sad tangos with lyrics that my father used to sing. Later in life as I was exposed to the dance, I embraced *milonguero*-style tango with its emphasis on close embrace. My taste in tango has changed over time. While I have studied figures and can follow when my partner creates distance to do them, I much prefer what is danced in tight spaces and in close embrace. I love dancing with the old *milongueros* who move, not just to the music, but also to the sentiment of the lyrics. For that reason I am partial to the matinee and early evening *milongas* at the clubs El Arranque, Canning, *Chiqué*, La Ideal, Gricel's, Centro Region Leonesa, and Lo de Celia, where many of the patrons are older and traditional in their dance. Information about each of these *milongas* and others will appear later in this chapter.

OVERVIEW OF THE TANGO SCENE

Scattered throughout BsAs, both within the capital district and the outlying areas, are as many as one hundred *milongas* every week. Every afternoon, evening, and night of the week you can dance from three or four in the afternoon until at least three or four in the morning, and sometimes later. For each time slot there are many choices about where to dance. The largest concentration of *milongas* can be found in the neighborhoods (*barrios*) in and around **El Centro**. That includes the *barrio* of **San Nicolás,** as well as the *barrios* of **Balvanera** or **Congreso.** In addition, the surrounding *barrios* of **San Telmo**, **Monserrat, San Cristobal**, **Constitución**, **Boedo**, **Almagro**, and **Palermo Soho** all have options for dancing. A complete listing of current *milongas* can be found in a number of publications, including *BA tango*, *Tangauta*, *La Milonga* and the *Tango Map*. The publications are described fully in the next section of this chapter. Addendum 4 includes an alphabetical listing of the dance halls that I am recommending, their addresses, and the days and nights on which they host *milongas*.

It is easy to get lost in the long list of *milongas* that appear in the magazines. However, not all *milongas* are equal. *Milongas* generally become popular, not because of their location or their lack of competition, but by the reputation of their organizers, the music the DJs play, and the level of dancing of their patrons. For example, La Ideal, one of the better-known spots, fills to capacity on Sunday afternoons when Paula and Carlos run their *milonga*. It is well attended by both locals and tourists and is centrally located. On the other hand, the Saturday night *milonga* held at the same club, La Ideal, does not have the same draw, even when it offers a show.

Milongas and their popularity change constantly. Places that are popular one month or season may not be the next month or season. In addition, what is a great *milonga* for one person may be dismal for another. Some dancers prefer large spaces, lots of people, and young dancers; while others opt for more intimate spaces, less crowding, and older dancers. I have had some of my best dances at poorly attended *milongas*. Large crowds do not always guarantee the best dancing, nor do they afford the best opportunity to be asked to dance.

Personally, I don't always go to *milongas* to dance. Sometimes I go just to listen to the music, observe the dancers, and soak in the culture. I watch in order to learn and to develop my dance and music palate. I may even pick up a new embellishment, a form of embrace, or the way individuals personalize their dance.

By and large, fancy figures are not seen on crowded dance floors. At a crowded *milonga*, figures can be dangerous to couples dancing around you. Certainly *boleos* and steps that separate your feet from the floor are especially dangerous. What is in vogue in BsAs is walking beautifully to the music (*al compás*). However, some *milongas* actually encourage both fancy figures and experimentation. For example, La Viruta, a popular club among the younger set, teaches such moves in classes that are offered right before their official *milonga* begins.

As already noted, an elegant walk, rather than a variety of figures, is the mark of good dancing in BsAs. This is most obvious at the annual World Championship Tango Competition (*Campeonato Mundial*) held in BsAs in August. On the surface, everyone dances beautifully, and to the untrained eye the differences between couples seem insignificant. However to the trained eye, and the judges, differences are present. All competitors in the category of *Tango Salón* dance simply, and never disconnect from their partners. Dancers are judged by their walk, first and foremost. They are also judged by their style, their elegance, their musicality (couple's rhythm and ability to dance in harmony with the music), the sentiment with which they dance, and their connection to their partners—not by doing fancy figures. In the *milongas* of BsAs, fancy figures generally identify a foreigner or novice.

TANGO PUBLICATIONS

As noted in the first section of this book, there are at least four free major monthly tango publications that list tango venues, usually by day and time. **Tangauta** and **BA Tango** are the most popular. Both are bilingual publications. Unfortunately, they often come out late into the month. **La Milonga** is the newest addition to tango publications. All three are glossy magazines with a great deal of information and advertising related to tango, including ads, pictures taken at local *milongas*, announcements of special events and performances, as well as lists of *milongas*, practice sessions (*prácticas*), and classes (*clases*). The startup time for events is generally written as a twenty-four-hour clock. Therefore, twenty-two hours (*horas*) is the equivalent of 10:00 PM.

BA Tango also produces a small tri-monthly guide to the *milongas*. It is published separately and in a format that is easy to carry around in your shoe bag or pocket.

A lesser known publication **La Porteña Tango**, offers yet another source of information about the tango scene in BsAs. It is in newspaper format, written exclusively in Spanish, and includes articles of musical historical interest. It is wonderful for those who want to read articles in Spanish about the tango heroes, e.g., songwriters, singers, and musicians. The last section is entitled *"Tangomovida del mes"* ("The Tango scene of the month"). It lists shows, open mike clubs, and dinner clubs (*espectáculos* and *tango-cena* shows), as well as tango academies, some lesser known *milongas*, museums (*museos*), TV specials, and classes for dance, folklore, and song.

Most of these publications are available at the entrance to *milongas*, where your ticket is purchased. Some of the shoe stores also carry these free guides.

GENERAL INFORMATION ABOUT CLUBS

In December of 2004 a fire broke out at a rock concert at the Cromagnon Club in downtown BsAs. One hundred and ninety-four young people died in the blaze. The fire resulted in the closure of many clubs, including some *milongas* throughout the city that were not up to code. Slowly but surely the clubs were reopened, once they could show that they had the necessary safety measures in place. As a result, some of the more popular clubs now close their doors when they reach their capacity, for fear of being closed down. It therefore pays to go early to the most popular *milongas*. This is especially true for La Ideal and Lo de Celia on Sunday afternoons/early evenings. In addition, smoking was banned from all clubs. Those who wish to smoke go outside or, in some cases, smoke in a separate room (e.g., at El Arranque).

When to Arrive

Generally speaking, it is not a bad idea to arrive early, i.e., close to when the club opens, or to get there after the big crunch in order to be well-seated and seen. Otherwise, it is easy to get lost in the crowd. Your chances of being asked to dance during these off times are enhanced. But also know that men (and women) sometimes come early to dance before heading home to their spouses or partners (and I don't mean dance partners).

On the subject of partners and dates, Saturday **night** is usually date night. If you are a woman traveling alone, you would do well going to a movie or a show on Saturday night. On the other hand, Saturday **afternoon** is a good opportunity for singles to dance. There are a number of very popular *milongas* that begin after 3:00 PM and end by 9:00 PM or 10:00 PM.

The big Saturday night exception is Club Sunderland (Lugones 3161). It is worth going there, even if you don't have a partner or don't dance. And you probably won't dance, if you are a woman traveling alone. However, you will see the most authentic dancing and shows. If you arrive early (around 10:00 PM), you can have dinner in the small restaurant at the entrance or inside the club. Sunderland is the ultimate tango experience. Go and enjoy the atmosphere: an old social club and gym. It will take you back in time and give you a glimpse of what was then.

Be prepared for a long cab ride out to Villa Urquiza, a distant *barrio* outside of the capital district of BsAs. From downtown, it might take approximately a half hour, if the driver knows exactly where he is going, and it will cost around 35 *pesos* or about $10. In taking a *remis* or radio-taxi, it would be prudent to have your tango map with you, just in case the driver has trouble finding the exact street. A small flashlight will also enable you or the driver to read the small print at night.

Reservations

Reservations are recommended for Friday and Saturday night *milongas*, unless you arrive early. Seats should also be reserved at *milongas* that are very popular (e.g., La Ideal on Sunday afternoon or Centro Región Leonesa on Saturday afternoon afternoon or Gricel's on Monday or Friday nights, among others). Reservations are also recommended where there is live music and/or entertainment or exhibition dancing (e.g., Parakultural at Canning on Fridays and Saturdays). In addition, if you are with a few friends, reservations are a good idea. Singletons can be accommodated at an overbooked *milonga* more easily than groups, and as a single person, expect to be seated with people you have never met.

Some tables are reserved for regular patrons or individuals who have called in a reservation. Reserved tables are dispersed after a defined wait time, and each establishment has its own policy about how and when reserved tables can be released.

Some clubs will always create room at choice tables for well-known dancers as well as for good dancers, even without reservations. Going frequently to the same club may also ensure preferential seating.

The Layout of Clubs and Seating Patterns

Seating is divided into sections: a section for couples, a section for single men (i.e., men who are without partners), and a section for single women. That sometimes means that women are on one side of a room and men are on the other side (e.g., *Chiqué*, Plaza Bohemia). Some clubs mix men and women, but at contiguous tables, rather than at the same table (e.g., Gricel's, Canning). It is usually easy to spot couples at a club, since they are always seated in a separate section. Remember that if you are seated as a couple, there is no possibility of you dancing with others. If you have traveled with your spouse or partner, but want to dance with the locals, you must ask to be seated separately and it is probably even wiser to enter the club separately.

Air Quality

All clubs have recently been designated as smoke-free, a ruling that is being strictly enforced. Smokers step outside the club to smoke or go to a separate room. In addition, most clubs are now air conditioned in the summer (December–March).

Food

The food sold at *milongas* is light fare, with an emphasis on drinks. There are non-alcoholic beverages served including bottled water with or without gas *(agua con gas or agua sin gas)*, seltzer *(soda)*, and bottled or canned soda *(gaseosa)*. As for alcoholic beverages, wine *(vino)* and beer *(cerveza)* are available. Hard liquor is also available, but very expensive. Don't think of asking for mixed fancy drinks. If they are served, you will probably be disappointed. By and large, people go to *milongas* to dance rather than drink.

Also available are finger foods such as *tostadas* (thin toasted sandwiches), *migas* (thin sandwiches on white bread), and chicken or meat pies *(empanadas de pollo or empanadas de carne)*. (See Chapter 2 for descriptions.) In some clubs, pizza is available. Sunderland is one of the few clubs that offers a full dinner menu. However, patrons usually arrive early to eat and many choose to eat in the adjoining restaurant rather than at their dance table.

Bathroom Facilities

Most women's bathrooms *(baño de damas/mujeres)* at *milongas* have an attendant who doles out toilet paper, hand towels, and also sells personal toiletries. Some even sell clothing. It is a good idea to carry change *(monedas)* with you, so that you can tip the attendant.

Stalls are generally equipped with small garbage cans for toilet paper. Because of the age of the plumbing in many of the old buildings, patrons are asked to place used toilet paper in these receptacles in order to prevent the clogging of pipes.

BEHAVIOR AT *MILONGAS*

Seating

As noted in the previous section under Reservations, all clubs have tables and assigned seating. However, seating patterns differ by club. Gricel's, for example, separates men and women by table but does not place them in different parts of the room. *Chiqué*, on the other hand, seats women on one side of the room and men on the other. In addition, there is a pecking order. When a club knows a patron, his/her seat may be reserved automatically, even if the party had not made formal reservations. In addition, women who are known by the host/hostess to be good dancers are placed, if possible, on the front lines at some clubs.

As for seating, you must **wait to be seated**. A host/hostess will greet you at the entrance and seat you, or assign you to a waiter for seating. You may request a particular area, e.g., close to the dance floor, in the middle of the section for women, or close to a wall with a wide view of the seating area. Where you sit is very important since some seats give you better visual access to possible dance partners. It is not surprising to be seated at a table where you do not know anyone.

As a single man or woman, **make note of the layout of the room** and the seating of the sexes before being seated. Note the best sections for you to be seen, to see, and to make eye contact with the greatest number of people of the opposite sex. That sometimes means that sitting right next to the dance floor may not be good, since you would have to be constantly turning around to catch someone's eye or to see who is trying to make eye contact with you. This is especially true at El

Arranque. However, if you are there to look at the dancers close up or to listen to the music, a front row seat may be perfect. (See discussion under The Invitation to Dance.) If the room is long and narrow, as in Gricel's, you will probably not get a front row seat, since they are generally reserved for their regular patrons.

It is customary and good etiquette when seated to greet your table partners. If a connection was made during the *milonga*, it is also appropriate to kiss them good-bye. Generally, women (and men) are friendly and some are very interested in practicing English. This might be a time to elicit advice about good *milongas* (*las mejores milongas*) and/or teachers (*los mejores maestros*).

The one time that talking is not a good idea is right before a dance set (*tanda*) begins (to be described below). That is when seeking out a partner becomes a serious business, and should have no distractions. At a table, a friend of mine was told by her table partners, "OK, ladies, let's go to work."

Changing Shoes

If you have brought dance shoes, you will want to change them before dancing. For women, this is often done in the ladies room and, less frequently, discreetly at the table. Men do not usually change shoes at a *milonga*. They go dressed wearing the shoes they will use to dance. Changing shoes for men is generally the mark of a foreigner.

First Observe

Once seated, **look at the dancers** to see whom you might want to dance with. Look at their embrace and their walk, and notice the cadence, posture, and sentiment of potential partners.

As anxious as you may be to dance, inviting or accepting an invitation from someone you have not seen dance may not be a good idea. The person might not be a good dancer and may make you look bad, resulting in you not dancing the rest of the night. **Declining an invitation is done discreetly by avoiding eye contact**. When you are new to the club, take your time and relish the variety of dancing styles, and the ways in which men negotiate packed dance floors. Notice how men mark time, waiting for an open space in which to move. Observe the subtle ways in which women embellish their walks, and the way couples use pauses, keep time, and mark rhythm, even as they stand seemingly motionless on the floor.

And women will, of course, want to take note of the way that other women adorn their bodies, feet, and hair. Men may want to focus on the way in which *milongueros* dress up, even as they dress down. In a crowded room, you will see men in slacks and sport shirts next to men in suits and ties. You will see women in jeans next to women in formal dress. Some show a great deal of skin, while others dress more modestly. You will see dance sneakers next to elegantly sandaled feet. Eventually, most women get asked to dance, regardless of their dress, but pay special attention to those individuals who are constantly on the dance floor. What is the key? Is it beautiful dancing, fancy figures, or sexy attire? Or is it some combination? Emulate the best in dance and dress, while retaining that which makes you and your dancing unique.

The Invitation to Dance

The nod of the head *(cabeceo)*, the wink on an eye, or raised eyebrows across a room is the way than men signal their intention to dance with a woman. It is, therefore, important for a woman to be seated in a position that allows her to scan the sea of single men, and to keep her eyes moving across them to see who may be trying to make eye contact with her. There are women (and men) who caution against constant scanning, since it may not give men the opportunity to connect with you. You need to see what works for you at different clubs. While women should **NEVER** ask men to dance, at least not directly; women can sustain eye contact with a man. This may result in catching his eye and being asked to dance.

The *cabeceo* is both polite and forgiving, allowing both men and women to save face and to dance only with partners they feel are compatible. Make your invitation as a man, or your rejection as a woman, as subtle as possible so as to avoid mutual embarrassment. Rejection should be made discreetly, so that as few people as possible are aware of the transaction. Making a face or wagging a finger in rejection is not subtle, but turning your head or eyes in another direction is.

Once you receive and acknowledge a man's *cabeceo*, do not, I repeat **DO NOT, stand up or walk to meet your prospective partner**. And men should not walk across a crowded dance floor to meet their partner, but rather along its periphery. Women should wait until the man has come close to her table, whereby she knows unequivocally that he has chosen her to dance. As a woman, I have been embarrassed more than once by standing up and walking towards my partner too soon, only to find him walk past me to dance with the woman seated next to or behind me.

Equally, a man should not go up to a table and ask a woman to dance. There is no saving face if a woman refuses his invitation. Generally, if a woman has not seen a man dance, she will refuse his invitation. I have known Argentine women who turn the refusal into a reprimand.

As a woman, your chances for being asked to dance can be enhanced by getting up and walking around the room, or at least to the ladies room. What you wear from the waist up (color, jewelry, hair ornamentation) will help men remember you when you sit back down. If you are not dancing, listen to the music with feeling and appreciation, and let your pleasure at being there show on your face. I have had men comment to me on my smile, saying that it was in stark contrast to other women, and one of the reasons they wanted to dance with me. The lesson is, even if you feel bored or angry, try not to show it.

There is an exception to the "never ask men to dance" rule. At **some** practice sessions (*prácticas*), women are discouraged from sitting and watching. Hosts want to see everyone dancing. It is the one time that women are encouraged to ask a man to dance. This releases the teacher or host from being responsible for everyone dancing. The *practica* at La Ideal is one such example. Diego and Zoraida run a wonderful practice session on Tuesdays and Fridays from 12:00 PM–3:00 PM. It targets new dancers, but also supports old timers who want to practice during the day. In their promotional literature Diego and Zoraida state:

> In contrast to the *milonga*, women can and should ask men to dance in order to take advantage of the class/*practica*. The golden rule is to accept all invitations. (English translation)

Your First Tango

Women should be selective in accepting their first tango since it is their debut. It affords onlookers the opportunity to see how you dance and to decide whether or not they want to dance with you. If you have the luxury, wait to dance to music that moves you, a favorite tango or orchestra. Good partners recognize when a woman feels the music.

Since eye contact from across a crowded dance floor is the way that men ask women to dance, both men and women should avoid eye contact with people with whom they do not want to dance. In deciding with whom you would like to dance your first tango, a woman should look for a man who walks beautifully and moves to the music. You also want someone who respects the line of dance, stays in his dancing lane, keeps his position in that lane, and maintains a safe space for himself and his partner. The men with whom I most enjoyed dancing did not rush the dance, nor did they pass couples ahead of them during the dance. If they found themselves behind a slow couple, they waited until one tango ended, and then moved up a few spaces, past the slow moving couple before the next tango began. Men may want to look for women who move in close communion with their partner, and who step with their partner and the music and not ahead of either.

Dance Sets (*Tandas*)

Music played in the *milongas* of BsAs are grouped and played in sets (*tandas*). Generally, one kind of music or one orchestra and/or singer defines the *tanda*. Each *tanda* consists of three to five pieces of like music. A set of DiSarli's tangos may be followed by a set of D'arienzo's tangos, and then by a set of Castillo's waltzes. Another set of tangos might follow, and then a *milonga* set. Over the course of an evening, there is usually a set dedicated to the *Chacarera*, an Argentinean folk dance. Men and women are quick to line up for this set. Some clubs may also play one set of Latin/salsa music and/or a set of swing tunes, over the course of the *milonga*.

Once a man commits to a dance, he commits to all the dances within a *tanda*. Unless a man is rude or disrespectful, a woman never ends a *tanda* before the established time, nor does she leave a man on the dance floor. It is a kiss of death. Anyone who has seen you will take note and probably not ask you to dance. The polite way, or the least offensive way, to end a *tanda* early is to say that you are not feeling well (*No me siento bien*). Excuse yourself (*!Disculpe!*), and say you need to sit (*Tengo que sentarme*). Under no circumstance, do you accept another invitation to dance during that *tanda*.

Between *tandas*, the music changes. A short interlude is played (*cortina*), giving everyone the opportunity to walk off the floor. *Cortina* comes from the word curtain, as in curtain call, marking the end of the play or the end of a scene. During the *cortina*, the club might play folk music, swing, Latin, or a tango sung by Carlos Gardel, the tango icon, or a modern tango by Piazzola. *Milongueros* do not dance to Gardel or Piazzola, rather they listen to them. Therefore, it is not unusual for the DJ to play a portion of a tango by either as a *cortina*.

At the end of a *tanda*, the man generally follows or leads the woman back to her seat or at least to the aisle where she is seated. A new *tanda* begins once the floor is cleared.

DANCE FLOOR ETIQUETTE

The Embrace

In BsAs, *milongueros* do not begin dancing when the music begins. They wait until they hear the music and feel the muse, often after the prelude or beginning of the tango.

Once face-to-face with your partner on the dance floor, wait for the man to initiate the **embrace (*el abrazo)*.** As a woman, do not be too anxious to embrace your partner. For starters, *milongueros* do not generally start dancing on the first note or phrase. They listen to the music before initiating the embrace and starting to dance. They also do not always end the dance at the last note, but may end it sooner, or even after the last note is heard. Listen to their bodies and follow their lead, without anticipating either the beginning or the end of the dance. The dance begins as the man moves towards an embrace and ends when he breaks that connection. A partner once reminded me, that HE determines the end of a dance, and only then is the embrace broken. A delay by a man in breaking the embrace should therefore be taken as a compliment.

The Tempo and the Lead

Men also define the tempo and rhythm they will keep (*compás*). Some men will listen and dance to the beat and others to the melody. Some will respond to an instrument such as the violin, the *bandoneón*, or the piano. Other men might choose to dance to the singer.

A woman must take her cue from the man. As such, women should listen to their partner's body and the movement of his chest. As many of you may know, the man's upper torso is the clue as to when and how you move. Keep your chest connected to your partner at all times, unless of course he signals a separation in order to complete a move.

Be aware that the pace of the dance is slower in BsAs. In addition, *milongueros* rarely lose the beat (*compás*). While they always move to the music, they do not always step to or on every beat. Therefore, do not anticipate a move, even when you are familiar with a tango or with a dance sequence. *Milongueros* dance to the music and not to a sequence of choreographed moves. **WAIT** for the man to mark or signal the move. Enjoy the connection and learn to **wait, listen, and feel**, but also learn to put life and energy into your pauses. Observe the women who get asked to dance all the time. Even when their bodies are still, they have energy and are in motion, albeit subtle. (The concept of energy in pauses was discussed in some detail in the previous chapter.)

As a woman your responsibility in the dance is to feel (*sentir*) both what your partner is feeling and what he is hearing, and to respond (*responder*) without anticipating. In essence, the woman hears the music through the man's body. That does not mean that the woman has no say in this dance. For me, the dance is a silent communication between a man and a woman, with the woman attending to the man's interpretation of the music, just as he attends to hers. The biggest challenge for me was learning to slow down and to appreciate and actually revel in my partners' pauses and in their energy—the energy of silence.

Maneuvering around the Floor

Line of dance is very important in BsAs since floors are generally very crowded. Dancers move counterclockwise and are supposed to stay in the order and the lane in which they began dancing. Men do not pass nor should they allow the space in front of them to become large enough for a couple to move in unexpectedly. The latter may mean that you are holding up the others waiting in line behind you. However, as a man you need to allow enough space (a cushion) for the couple in front to take one step back. Nevertheless, back steps by a man can be dangerous since there is no assurance that another couple is not right on your heels. Therefore, it is best for men to avoid taking back steps, unless they have a way of avoiding a collision with couples behind them.

On crowded dance floors, which are the norm in BsAs, men need to learn to maneuver within a two-by-two square. Think of it as real estate that you are temporarily renting. The square becomes your holding pattern until another contiguous space or piece of real estate becomes available.

As a result, tango in Argentina is somewhat circular, rather than linear. It is full of pauses, but pauses with cadence and energy, not dead wait time. While a line of dance is followed, couples move into spaces and remain there moving in circular motion, e.g., doing *ochos cortados*, rocking steps, or simply changing weight; whatever enables the couple to remain in their two-by-two real estate, before moving on to the next plot of land when it is vacated.

All of this is necessitated by the fact that there is little room for moving forward on a crowded dance floor. And moving backwards is dangerous. To avoid accidents and embarrassment, always keep your feet on the floor. Avoid moves such as *boleos* and *ganchos* that could potentially injure couples in close proximity. Dance floors are very crowded and kicking or stepping on someone is another kiss of death.

Small Talk between and during Tangos

There is no talk (small or otherwise) during the dance. Talking is limited to what can be said between tangos and since tangos in a *tanda* meld into each other, there is little time for talk. However, since *milongueros* never start dancing at the beginning of a tango, there may be some space for talk. Between tangos, the conversation may revolve around where one comes from (*¿De dónde sos?*), or when one arrived (*¿Cuándo llegaste?*), or how long one may have been dancing (*¿Cuánto hace que bailás?*), or how long one is staying (*¿Cuánto tiempo te vas a quedar?*).

At the end of a *tanda* the woman might say thank you (*gracias*) or that she enjoyed dancing with you (*me gustó bailar con vos*). Saying g*racias* at the end of a tango (rather than at the end of a *tanda*) is generally meant to end a set, even if it is not the last tango in that set. A friend of mine was wondering why men walked away from her when she said *gracias* before the *tanda* ended. When a friend told her why men were leaving her before the set was over, she went around apologizing for the unintended end she had put to the set.

A woman should also not allow a man to sit at her table at the end of a *tanda*, or to accept a drink by a dance partner, unless of course, she has interests outside of the dance. Once other men see a woman seated with a man, they avoid eye contact out of respect for that man.

Staying Cool on and off the Floor

It is easy to get overheated when the room is full or after you have been dancing for a few straight sets. This is the time for men to take out their handkerchiefs (*pañuelo*), and women to take out their fans (*abanico*). *Milongueros* have traditionally used the handkerchief to dry the sweat on their faces, or alternatively, to place in their hands when they are dancing so as to keep the woman's hand dry. Men who perspire a great deal sometimes come with a change of shirt or undershirt, knowing that a sweaty shirt can be a turnoff for many women. Women may also carry handkerchiefs to dry their brow, or they may use a fan at their table. But sometimes the best remedy to staying cool is to pace your dancing and to sit out sets so that you can recompose for a set that you absolutely must dance.

Coming Back for More

The big question for me, as a woman, is what makes a man seek me or any other woman out again. You have followed flawlessly, or so you felt, never skipping a beat or equivocating. You danced with feeling for the music and with pleasure on your face. You thought the connection was great. So why did your partner, thereafter, avoid your gaze? In a quest for an answer, I asked some male friends both in BsAs and in NY what makes them come back for more.

Initially, men select partners because of a physical attraction or because the woman looks great on the dance floor. She seems relaxed, does not seem to be anticipating moves, steps on the beat, and appears to be into and enjoying her partner, rather than scanning the room for someone else while dancing. Men tell me that even when a woman looks good in the arms of another man, how she feels in his arms becomes more important. Men notice their partner's embrace, the woman's responsiveness to his lead and to the music, her connection to his body, and, most importantly, her lack of tension.

A friend once told me that the reason he stopped asking me to dance was because I hummed or sang as I danced. Shortly after that disclosure, another partner asked me why I no longer sang with the music. Clearly, the same behavior elicited very different responses. The moral of this story is that no one way is right. Personally, I love it when an Argentine sings to me while dancing, but then again, that is my taste.

MILONGAS

Sponsorship of *Milongas*

A single location, such as Plaza Bohemia (Maipu 444), can be the site of a different *milonga* every night, each organized by a different individual or couple, and each enjoying a different degree of popularity. Plaza Bohemia sponsors La Shusheta on Mondays, Sentimental y Coqueta on Tuesdays, El Maipú on Wednesdays early, and La Marshall, a gay-friendly *milonga* later the same night, among other *milongas* throughout the week.

Another example is Confitería Ideal (Suipacha 384), a popular spot with locals and tourists. It offers approximately eleven *milongas* and sixteen classes a week, some starting as early as noon. Different hosts sponsor the various practice sessions (*prácticas*) and *milongas* at La Ideal. Classes that precede *milongas* are also taught by a variety of teachers.

Because of the relative stability of *milongas*, listings in guidebooks published within the year are generally good resources to use in planning your trip. However, because of the occasional changes and additions to the *milonga* scene, some older guides may be incomplete or inaccurate. Organizers may suddenly drop one of their *milongas* or change its day or starting time, e.g., Lo de Celia, a very popular *milonga* recently dropped its early *milonga* on Saturday but kept its late *milonga* that same night. Therefore, it is important to check the most recent listing or publication for up-to-date information.

The *milongas* listed in this section are not intended to be all-inclusive. Comprehensive lists are available in the tango publications discussed earlier in this chapter. In this section,

I have highlighted the most popular *milongas*, closest to the center of town. They are the *milongas* that I most enjoyed and that were recommended by *milonguero* friends in BsAs, as well as friends from New York that often visit BsAs.

The recommendations have been divided into two sections: early *milongas* starting before 7:00 PM, and late *milongas* starting after 8:00 PM, more likely after 10:00 PM. Also listed for the early *milongas* are the *subte* lines and stations that leave you in closest proximity to the club. However, since the *subte* stops running around 10:00 PM, your return later at night must be by radio-taxi or bus. While bus service is slower at night, buses do run around the clock. Late night *milongas* are better and more safely accessed by radio-taxi. Often clubs will have taxis waiting outside for customers. These too are safe alternatives.

For easy reference, a summary of the *milongas* is found in two appendices. Addendum 2 charts *milongas* by day of week and start up time. Addendum 3 lists the dance halls alphabetically and includes their addresses and days of the week in which they sponsor *milongas*.

Early *Milongas*

Late afternoon and early evening *milongas* are generally frequented by a mature clientele (*gente grande*). While some may not always be the most accomplished dancers, they feel the music and their dancing shows it. They are the men with whom I most enjoy dancing. This is a description of the most popular spots and *milongas* where patrons can begin dancing early in the evening:

1) **Confitería La Ideal**   (Suipacha 384, near Av Corrientes; one flight up)
   Directions: *Subte* Line B to *Pellegrini* station or Line C to *Diagonal Norte* or Line D to *9 de Julio*

Schedule: Mondays, Wednesdays, Thursdays, Fridays, and Sundays beginning around 3:00 PM or 4:00 PM. A class precedes all afternoon *milongas*, except for the one held on Sunday afternoons.

La Ideal was built in 1912 and still carries the charm of that era with dark paneled walls, marble columns, wooden floors, and vintage lighting, albeit a bit worn. It represents the best of tango halls that graced Buenos Aires in the 1920s. The dance hall is one flight up. The ground floor serves as a confectionary, restaurant, and tearoom. One can still sit on the ground floor sipping tea, while listening to the strains of tango from the dance hall, one flight above. This is a popular spot for *porteños* and tourists alike. La Ideal has been featured in a number of movies including Robert Duval's *Assassination Tango* and Sally Potter's *The Tango Lesson*.

2) **Plaza Bohemia** (Maipu 444, near Av Corrientes; one flight up)
    Directions: *Subte* Line B to *Florida* station or Line C to *Lavalle*
    Schedule: Tuesdays the *milonga Sentimental y Coqueta* begins at 6:30 PM, and on Wednesdays *La Yumba* begins at 3:30 PM. A class precedes both *milongas*. On Friday, the early *milonga Milonguita del Centro* begins at 6:00 PM, and is also preceded by a class. While there is no class on Saturday, there is an early *milonga*, *Cachirulo*, that begins at 6:00 PM. Some of the early *milongas* at

Bohemia are followed by yet another *milonga* at night, with another sponsor/name.

Plaza Bohemia is a small space, both for seating and dancing. Because the dancing is good, the place gets packed very early in the evening, especially on Tuesdays. Early arrival or reservations are recommended.

3) **El Arranque** at the **Nuevo Salón La Argentina** (Bartolomé Mitre 1759, near Av Callao)
   Directions: *Subte* Line A to *Congreso* station or Line B to *Callao*
   Schedule: Mondays, Tuesdays, and Thursdays from 3:00 PM till 10:00 PM and on Saturdays from 3:00 PM till 9:00 PM

   El Arranque is a large space that gets packed on Mondays and Tuesdays. There is no class prior to their *milongas*. Periodically, there is live music and exhibition dancing.

4) *Chiqué* at **La Casa de Galicia** (San Jose 224, two blocks from Av de Mayo; one flight up)
   Directions: *Subte* Line A to *Saenz Peña* station
   Schedule: Thursdays from 4:00 PM–11:00 PM. A class precedes the *milonga*.

   Chiqué is another popular *milonga* with traditional seating of men on one side of the room and women on the other. Because the space is long and narrow, it is a good idea to try to be seated in the middle of the room, thereby having easier visual access to potential partners that are seated along the length of the room.

5) **Salón Canning** (Raul Scalabrini Ortiz 1331)
   Directions: Not easily accessible by *subte*. However, many buses cross Scalabrini Ortiz and Av Córdoba, just two short blocks from Canning.
   Schedule: The *milonga A Puro Tango* is held on Wednesdays from 4:00 PM till 11:00 PM, and on Sundays from 6:00 PM till midnight. A class precedes both *milongas*.

   Canning is a large square hall and a good place to see how men negotiate a very crowded floor. It is especially crowded between 6:00 PM and 8:30 PM. The size of the dance floor (*pista*) and the lighting make it hard to see who is signaling you to dance from across the floor—unless of course, you have eagle eyes. Nevertheless, it is worth the challenge.

6) **Centro Región Leonesa** (CRL) (Humberto Primo1462; one flight up)
   Directions: *Subte* Line E to *San Jose* station
   Schedule: La *milonga Entre Tango y Tango* on Wednesdays and Fridays begins at 6:00 PM. On Mondays there is a smaller *milonga*, *Mi Refugio*, starting at 6:30 PM and preceded by a class. The *milonga Los Consagrados* on Saturdays from 4:00 PM till 10:30 PM is also preceded by a class.

   CRL is a large and long space that also gets very crowded. As in *Chiqué*, women are seated on one side of the floor and men on the other. The difference is that there is more dancing floor space separating men and women. Once couples start dancing, it is hard to negotiate eye contact across the dancing crowd. Therefore, eye contact is important early on.

7) **Lo de Celia** (Humberto Primo 1783, corner of Entre Rios; one flight up)
Directions: *Subte* Line E to *Entre Rios* station
Schedule: Wednesdays and Sundays begins at 6:00 PM

Lo de Celia is a very popular *milonga* that attracts many *porteños* and good quality dancers. It is a square floor with women on two opposing sides of the square, and men on the other two sides. There are no classes or shows, just good dancing.

8) **El Beso** (Riobamba 416, near Av Corrientes; one flight up)
Directions: *Subte* Line B to Callao station
Schedule: Thursdays from 6:00 PM till 12:30 AM

El Beso attracts both the young and the not so young—generally all good dancers. The space is square and rather small, thereby easily crowded. It is located one flight up (*primer piso*).

Popular Nighttime *Milongas*

The *milongas* listed in this section generally begin after 8:00 PM, and most, closer to 10:00 PM. Some offer a class or two before the *milonga*. Given their late start-up time, it is advisable to take a radio-taxi to these spots. The *subte* system stops running around 10:00 PM. For this reason, directions are not included.

1) **La Ideal** (Suipacha 384), described under early *milongas*, also sponsors nightly *milongas* Tuesday through Saturday beginning around 10:30 PM. Most are preceded by a class or two. At least once or twice a week during nighttime *milongas*, there is live music and exhibition dancing.

2) **Canning** (Scalabrini Ortiz 1331) sponsors late *milongas* on Mondays, Tuesdays, Thursdays, Fridays, and Saturdays, beginning at 11:00 PM. It is a good place to take a class before their *milonga*. Usually, well-known teachers give the classes. In addition, Canning is ideal for visitors to observe how good dancers negotiate crowded spaces. Sometimes there are shows with exhibition dancing and live music. There is even a night that features old *milongueros* (*Noche de Milongueros*).

3) **Club Gricel** (La Rioja 1180, near Av San Juan) has *milongas* on Mondays at 8:30 PM, Thursdays at 8:00 PM, Fridays at 10:30 PM, Saturdays at 11:00 PM, and Sundays at 9:00 PM, all ending between 3:00 AM and 5:00 AM. Because the space is smaller (long rather than wide), it feels cozier than Canning. Nevertheless, it attracts good dancers and gets very crowded. On all nights, except Thursday, there is a class offered prior to

the *milonga*. In addition, there are classes sometimes offered on nights when there is no *milonga*.

4) **Plaza Bohemia** (Maipu 444) offers *milongas* on Mondays at 10:30 PM, Wednesdays at 11:00 PM, and Thursdays at 9:00. This small but popular *milonga* space fills to capacity on most early evenings and nights. On all nights, except Wednesday, there is a class offered. Wednesday night is a gay-friendly *milonga*.

5) **Niño Bien** at **Centro Región Leonesa Club** (Humberto Primo 1462, one flight up) runs a *milonga* on Thursdays beginning at 10:30 PM and is preceded by a class. Their *milonga* gets packed and reservations are important. At the very least, arrive early. In this way you are more likely to dance. The *milonga* ends at 4:00 AM.

6) **Porteño y Bailarín** (Riobamba 345, near Corrientes) sponsors *milongas* on Tuesdays and Sundays beginning at 10:00 PM, and is preceded by a class. The space in this club is small but the dancers are good, with the best dancers arriving really late. There is a section in the back where classes are given and where some dancers opt to sit during the *milonga*.

7) **El Beso** (Riobamba 416, near Av Corrientes) offers *milongas* on Tuesdays at 9:00 PM, Wednesdays at 10:30 PM, Saturdays at 11:00 PM, and Sundays at 10:00 PM. While the space is small, the club is very popular. There is a *milonguero*-style tango class offered before most *milongas*. It has a good reputation and is well attended. There is even class on some nights when there is no *milonga*. Again, veteran *milongueros* generally arrive late.

8) **Lo de Celia** (Humberto Primo 1783, near Av Entre
Rios) sponsors *milongas* on Fridays beginning at
10:00 PM and Saturdays beginning at 11:00 PM.
This is another very well attended *milonga*. While
reservations are recommended, the best seats are not
assured since they are reserved for regular patrons.
There are no classes offered here.

9) **Sueño Porteño** at **Boedo Tango** (Av San Juan 3330,
near Av Boedo) sponsors a *milonga* on Wednesdays
from 7:00 PM till 2:00 AM. This is a very popular
milonga that opened its doors in 2008. The space is
large with tables scattered in different sections of the
hall and a centrally located bar for additional seating.
This *milonga* begins early enough for *subte* access
(Line E to *Boedo* station). There is a class offered
beforehand. For 20 *pesos* you can take the class and
stay for the *milonga*. Reservations are not accepted
and people are seated on a first-come, first-served
basis.

10) **La Viruta** (Armenia 1366) is open on Wednesdays
through Sundays, beginning at midnight. This
is a late-night spot for the young set as well as for
milongueros who did not get enough dancing at
their previous club. It is a place to see good dancers,
especially after 2:00 AM. There are often featured
performers. *Milongas* are preceded by multilevel
classes, which focus on *nuevo tango*.

11) **La Baldosa** at **Salón El Pial** (Ramón Falcón 2750,
around Rivadavia 7200; off the beaten path, but
worth the trip). Their Friday night *milonga* begins
at 10:30 PM and includes exhibition dancing, and at

times live music. There is a class that begins about 8:30 PM before the *milonga*.

12) **Sunderland** (Lugones 3161) This very popular Saturday night *milonga* runs from 10:00 PM till 4:30 AM, and offers a show featuring traditional salon tango. A taxi ride to Sunderland may take as long as half an hour and cost around 55 pesos. Reservations are highly recommended (call 4541-9776) since you will sometimes get groups that are transported by bus filling the space. It is a great place for watching good classic dancers. As such, get there early and try to get a table with a view (highly unlikely, but go for it). Since this is date night it is also unlikely that you will dance. But then again, you may get lucky. Observing and relishing this old historic gym is half the fun. This is a cathedral of tango.

13) **Sin Rumbo** (Jose Tamborini 6157). Another off the beaten track *milonga* that is worth the trip. This too is a cathedral of tango with a long history. It is located in an outlying area of the capital district of BsAs. Because it is much smaller than Sunderland, you can see the dancing better. It too has a long history. Reserve a table close to the dance floor, if possible. The dancers that frequent this club represent the distinctive style of *barrio urquiza*.

A CLOSING NOTE

I go to Buenos Aires for two reasons. First and foremost, I go to dance. And secondly, I go to feel good about myself, as well as my dancing.

It is for the latter reason that I choose milongas that affirm me as a mature woman and as a dancer. Milongas that affirm both my dancing and me are where I can shine, get asked to dance often, and where I dance as well as if not better than many. I avoid places where everyone is much younger, bold in their dress, and/or doing fancy figures. If I am feeling secure, I may go to a milonga that can push my dancing to another level—a bit outside of my comfort zone, and that presents a challenge that I am up to, or where I can learn by observing.

While dancing within my comfort zone gives me confidence, it does not stretch me. Confidence, however, does serve me well in that it lowers my inhibitions and enables me to take risks. When I leave my comfort zone and enter a zone of discomfort, my persona changes, as does my dancing. I tense up, my body does not respond naturally, and I obsess about form. That is when I return to the places where I feel secure.

After all, I am in Buenos Aires to enjoy myself and to dance with abandon.

MAY YOU TOO DANCE WITH ABANDON!

Chapter 5
Learning about Tango: Entertainment and History

"El tango es un sentimiento triste que se baila"
(Tango is a sad sentiment to which you dance.)
Enrique Santos Discepolo

I sat in the theater with tears in my eyes. On stage were thirty-five musicians, including twelve string instruments and four bandoneónes. The orchestra played tangos I had heard in the *milongas*, but what touched me most were the tangos my father played when I was a child—*Caminito* and *La Cumparsita*—all this for free on a weekday afternoon.

Personal BA Journal
November 2008

The possibilities for learning about tango in BsAs are endless. You can learn from the music directly, but you can also learn from the institutions that support and preserve tango throughout the city. Opportunities to hear tango begin at home, i.e., your residence. You can wake up to tango on radio or TV. My biggest pleasure was being able to cook, eat, dress, and fall asleep to tango—its music, interviews, shows, instructional videos, and exhibition dancing—all at the touch of a button. And then you can see and hear tango on the streets, in the *subte* stations, in the museums, cultural centers, street fairs, concert halls, theaters, and, of course, in the local bars. On every corner of BsAs you are reminded that this is the city that exudes tango.

OVERVIEW

Throughout the city there are many venues through which tango music and dance can be heard and seen. Some venues target tourists, offering a costly **dinner and show** (*cena* show). This is "tango for export" (*tango fantasía*), as noted by the locals, but for locals the prices are prohibitive. More importantly, this is not what the locals generally would choose, even if they had the resources to do so. More reasonable venues, and in some cases more authentic ones, are **restaurants** that during the day offer a regular menu but on select nights include a show where dinner is optional and à la carte. In these places there is usually a cover charge (*cubierto*) for the entertainment and a minimum (*un mínimo*) that must be spent on food and/ or drinks. The entertainment may include a few singers, live musical accompaniment, and a dancer or two. Both options are covered in Chapter 2: Dining with Tango.

The purpose of this chapter is to describe the places where tango is available in BsAs outside of the aforementioned venues; where the music can be heard live and up close, intimate bars where local patrons are moved to silence, and some even to tears, and concert halls and theaters that cater to the *porteño*. The chapter is also intended to share where the most authentic salon dancing can be seen. And finally, it will inform the reader about where to learn about tango—both its history and the musicians that gave it life and who, even after death, continue to live on the dance floors of BsAs.

The most authentic venues for hearing tango are the traditional and sometimes historic bars, alternatively referred to as **tango bars and clubs**. They offer their patrons the opportunity to hear tango as they drink or snack at the cost of what is consumed. In this venue, entertainment is king. Food, if available, is an afterthought. Some nights might feature an open mike (*micrófono abierto/peña*) for aspiring performers impassioned by tango.

Music and dance shows can also be found in the equivalent of large **Broadway-like theaters**, many on *Calle Corrientes*. In these theaters, you will see all forms of tango— from the traditional to the avant-garde, from singers with simple musical accompaniment to dramatic instrumentals, and from small groups to full orchestras. More intimate and inexpensive shows are offered at the **cultural centers** (*centros culturales*), **museums** (*museos*), and **government buildings** scattered throughout the city. Government-subsidized events are generally free (*libre y gratuita*) or they may charge a small fee.

Finally, there are the *milongas* that regularly feature dance exhibitions by old and young *milongueros* for the price of entry into the *milonga*. Some even offer live music, as was the case at the *milongas* of the 1940s. *Milongas* are, by far, the most authentic and least expensive venues for seeing and hearing live tango. Performances at *milongas* are generally advertised in flyers (*volantes*) distributed at the clubs and in ads found in the monthly tango publications *BA Tango*, *Tangauta*, *La Milonga*, and/or *La Porteña Tango*.

This chapter begins with a brief description of the role that tango music and dance played over time in the shaping of a *milonguero*. The rest of the chapter is divided into the five aforementioned venues where authentic music and dance can be seen and heard: **tango bars, theaters, cultural centers,**

governments sponsored events, and *milongas*, with options listed for each. Also included in this chapter are **museums** that not only provide historical information about tango, but may also offer shows to attract visitors. The chapter ends with the radio and TV media that is available twenty-four/seven.

What all of this means is that in Buenos Aires one can fall asleep and wake up to tango, while sipping tango throughout the day.

MUSIC AND DANCE IN THE LIVES OF *PORTEÑOS*

Over the course of my time in BsAs, I spoke to many *milongueros*, trying to understand how and when they learned to dance. It soon became obvious to me that most *milongueros* developed their sensitivity to the music and their skill in dancing by looking at and listening to tango—at home, at family parties and local *milongas*, and in neighborhood bars. Some watched for years before dancing. They reveled in the fine differences among great *milongueros*. They not only listened to the music, they immersed themselves in the sentiment that the instruments, voices, and lyrics expressed, and they took that sentiment to the dance floor. *Milongueros* wear that sentiment on their faces, in the way they listen to the music as they dance, the way they interpret that music, and on how and when they mark the rhythm (*como llevan el compás*).

Even when they don't dance, lovers of tango appreciate the tapestry of musicians who weave the different instruments into a whole, never losing their individual voices and identities. You don't really have to dance to be able to appreciate the music, and even the dance. This is most obvious in August, when *porteños* go en masse to see the international tango competitions for salon and stage tango. They stand in line long before 10:00 AM when the distribution of free tickets begins for the nighttime show. Not all attending this event are dancers, but all are lovers of the dance and the music. Because of the pervasiveness of tango music throughout BsAs, dancers and non-dancers alike often know the orchestras, the singers, the lyrics, and even some of the history of this music.

Over the years, I have given thought to the way that dancers outside of BsAs, myself included, develop their skills and perfect their craft. I started by **studying** the dance, i.e., taking classes. Most of us began that way. I also **observed** good dancers to figure out what distinguished them from others. Of course, I **practiced** whenever I had the chance in studios or in my home with selected partners, and even as I waited for elevators, or pushed my cart in the supermarket.

In reality, the classes with which I started my tango journey are an exception for the *milonguero*. Many have never studied this dance formally and yet they dance with incredible feeling. Over time, I have come to realize that really hearing the music, the instruments, the voices, and knowing the stories and poetry of this art form are what propel my dance forward, more than most other ways. This exposure and understanding has given my dance soul. *Porteños* have told me that I feel the music (*sentís la música*).

So where do *milongueros* go to watch their peers dance socially? And where do they go to listen to the music, without the distraction of the dance? And finally, where do they learn about the evolution and the icons of tango? This chapter will highlight the many opportunities that BsAs offers visitors and citizens alike, to hear and see authentic tango and to learn about its protagonists and its history.

GETTING THE FACTS ABOUT WHERE TO GO

The best way to find a comprehensive listing of restaurants, theaters and cafés that are currently offering commercial tango shows is to consult the entertainment section (*"Espectáculos"*) of the daily Spanish newspapers (*diarios*), *Clarín* or *La Nación*. On the last pages under Entertainment Guide (*cartelera*) and more specifically under Theater (*teatro*) are listings for restaurant/concert, music hall, and *bailes/copas* (dances/drinks). Clubs appear in alphabetical order and if your Spanish is limited just look for the word tango to find out where to hear and/or see tango on stage. Friday editions have a pull out section for "*Recomendados del fin de semana*" (Weekend recommendations) that lists tango events under "*música*" and then "tango."

In addition, many locales now have their own Web sites. They allow you to enter their doors electronically, look at their menus, even hear some of their featured musicians, and see who is currently appearing.

The *Buenos Aires Herald* is the English language newspaper that also lists some tango events in the "Get Out" section of their paper. You can get a free trial subscription to their paper for one month by logging on to http://www.buenosairesherald.com and registering.

Another source for current cultural events is a free weekly publication called *Cultura BA*. It is published by the Minister of Culture of BsAs and can be picked up on Thursdays either at the Teatro General San Martín on *Av Corrientes* 1530 or at Casa de la Cultura on *Av de Mayo* 575. It is difficult to read unless you understand Spanish since there is a great deal of text and entries are tightly packed into columns. However, by looking under "*museos*" or "*música popular*" you will find listings related to tango. The last page of this weekly offers readers instructions on how to get to the places by public transportation, under *¿Cómo llego?* (How do I get there?).

There is also a government Web site, http://www.cultura.gov.ar/agenda, that will give you current information about government-sponsored tango events, among other offerings. Look under music (*música*) or dance (*danza*).

However, the listings in these daily and weekly publications are incomplete. Many small bars only advertise their shows on flyers distributed at their locales. Sometimes they may not know who will be performing until a few days before an event. Some small bars have a strong local following. They are not looking for tourists to fill their space; so mainstream advertising is not essential.

Some of the smaller tango venues advertise in the monthly tango publications *BA Tango, Tangauta* and *La Porteña Tango*. The problem with these monthly publications is that they often come out late in the month, after shows have had their run. *La Porteña Tango* is somewhat timelier. Its last page has a section entitled "*Tangomovida de [Mes]*" ("Tango venues for [name of month]"). The shows listed under "*Espectáculos*" focus exclusively on tango so that you do not have to guess whether the entertainers are tango performers.

In addition to the word tango as a signal of a tango show, there are specific entertainers who dominate the tango circuit and draw the most locals. They include, but are not limited to, Susana Rinaldi, Adriana Varela, Lydia Borda, and Chino Laborde (singers), Leopoldo Federico, Raul Jaurena, Ruben Juarez, Nestor Marconi, Julio Pane, (*bandeonistas*), Juanjo Dominguez (guitarist), Horacio Salgan (pianist), Color Tango, El Arranque, Fernandez Fierro, Los Reyes del Tango, Nuevo Quinteto Real, and Sans Souci (orchestras)—to mention but a few.

TANGO VENUES DESCRIBED

Tango Bars/*Peñas*

Intimate bars that feature tango music as their main menu are scattered all around BsAs. Some advertise shows with well-known tango singers and/or dancers. Others have an open mike (*micrófono abierto/peña*) once or twice a week, with a guitarist and/or a keyboardist who can accompany any tango and voice range that is indicated to them right before the performance. Some *peña* performers will choose to recite a poem or whistle a tango. At some bars and social clubs you can eat a full meal, albeit from a limited menu, usually before the performance. At others, the fare is light with drinks as the standard accompaniment to the music. In all of these listings, the emphasis is on the music.

These bars and clubs are for individuals who want to see the most authentic tango performers as they connect to this soulful music. By and large, patrons know the language, and relish the sentiment of the music and the performers. However, even for those who do not understand the lyrics, the sentiment behind them is obvious from the intensity with which the music is played/sung, and the silence and facial expression of the patrons. This audience does not need a full complement of musicians and dancers to be entertained. In fact, patrons often look for venues where dancing does not detract from the music, but rather where music is king. These spaces are intimate. Nowhere is this more obvious than in the bars that place entertainers at a finger's distance from you. In this setting, you can clearly see the pathos in the faces of musicians as they play or sing. Understanding, or at least appreciating, that sentiment is important to the dance. It is what generally differentiates the milongueros' connection to the music from the foreigners' connection.

At some of these bars there is a cover charge (*cubierto*). At others, donations are solicited by passing a hat. At all, there is an expectation that you will have a few drinks.

Times and prices, if known, have been provided for listings. However, both times and prices are subject to modification without prior notice. It is best to check online or in the daily papers for details.

Amaycha Bar
Anchorena 628-632 (Bo Abasto)

Tel: 4865-7385

http://www.baramaycha.com.ar

This intimate Bohemian bar/restaurant is a local social club that offers tango shows on some nights. A hat is passed at the end of the performance for contributions to the entertainers. The restaurant serves a very limited menu of homemade food. I visited on a Wednesday night and took a class in *canyengue* tango in their backroom. Other classes are offered on Thursday and Saturday evenings.

Bien Bohemio
Sanchez de Loria 745 (near Boedo and Independencia) (Bo. Boedo)
Tel: 4957-1895

http://www.bienbohemiobar.com.ar

This was the home of Titi Rossi, bandeonista and author of tangos, including *Bien Bohemio*. His home was a bohemian hangout for musicians in the 1940s. After seventy years, Bien Bohemio continues to serve tango aficionados with shows from Thursday thru Sunday.

Saturday night is their formal show. On the three remaining nights, shows vary and may include an open mike (*peña*) for tango lovers. In addition, the café is open after 5:00 PM as a coffee house (*café*), and tango classes are offered on Thursdays before their weekly *peña*. Call or check online to verify performances.

Bien Porteño
Rivadavia 1392 (Bo. Centro)
Tel: 4383-5426

http://www.bienporteno.com

This café-bar offers tango shows on Friday and Saturday nights beginning around 10:00 PM. It also has an art gallery, *milongas* on some nights, and offers daily tango classes. Lunch and dinner are available.

Boliche de Roberto (officially registered as 12 de Octubre) (Bo. Almagro)
Bulnes 331, corner of Peron

This historic bar (*bar notable*) has no name on the outside but is locally referred to by its owner's name, Roberto. Inside is a bar, six small tables that seat up to four people each, and old and dusty wine bottles lining the walls.

This small and seedy bar dates back to 1930. What it lacks in luxury, it makes up for in sentiment—both on the part of the entertainers and the audience. Once the music begins many more patrons are squeezed in (standing room only) and then silence ensues. Singers often accompany themselves on guitar. The place is usually packed from just before midnight to the early hours of the morning with a young college-aged crowd that has come to see both old and young musicians play and sing tangos. One never knows who will be singing. This is the essence of a true *peña*. At the end of each performance, a hat is passed around for making contributions to the performers. Generally, show nights are Wednesdays thru Saturdays.

Café Montserrat
San Jose 524 (Bo. Monserrat)
Tel: 4381-2588
http://www.cafemontserrat.com

This is a charming, intimate bohemian café-bar with a changing art exhibit and live music, poetry readings, and other literary events. Musical shows held up to four nights a week feature folk, jazz, or tango musicians, with an open-mike (*peña*) on some nights. Starting time varies and on some nights there are two shows. A monthly calendar of performances is available at the café. Some events are free (*libre y gratuita*), and for others there is a cover charge (*cubierto*) of up to 20 *pesos* and a minimum consumption (*mínimo*) of 10 *pesos*. During the day, the café serves a light breakfast and lunch, as well as drinks.

Clásica y Moderna
Callao 892 (between Córdoba and Paraguay) (Bo. Norte)
Tel: 4812-8707
http://www.Clasicaymoderna.com
This is another notable bar dating back to 1938. It is a charming and intimate pub, with a small bookstore in the back. There is live music six nights a week, with many shows focused on tango. For a cover charge of 20–40 *pesos* (depending on the artist) and a minimum of 15–25 *pesos*, you can enjoy a two-hour show. The restaurant advertises its monthly schedule on a postcard of the bar.

El Balcón de la Plaza
Humberto Primo 461 (Bo. San Telmo)
Tel: 4362-2354
http://www.elbalcondelaplaza.com.ar
This tourist spot overlooks Plaza Dorrego in San Telmo. On Sundays, the restaurant is packed with tourists who want a ringside seat to the antique fair and to the tango exhibition dancing of *El Indio*. Inside, also on Sundays, the restaurant offers a show of continuous music and dancing for its patrons from 1:00 PM till 7:00 PM. On weekends, the restaurant hosts a *cena* show.

Fervido
México 1314 (Bo. San Telmo)
This intimate restaurant only opens on nights when there is a show or an open mike (peña), generally Saturdays and Sundays. The peña allows those who sign up that night to sing two or three tangos.

Musical accompaniment for participants takes the form of a keyboardist or guitarist(s). The menu is limited, but a meal can be ordered, as well as drinks and dessert.

La Casa del Tango
Guardia Vieja 4049 (near Calle Medrano and Corrientes) (Bo. Almagro)
Tel: 4963-6442/4863-0463 (Reservations are not needed)

On Wednesdays and Saturdays tango aficionados sign up to either sing two tangos or recite two poems. One never knows who will sing or the quality of what will be heard, but sentiment is never lacking. Two or three guitarists and sometimes a keyboardist accompany the performers. Here you will hear tangos you have probably never heard before. The *Peña de los Cantores* (singers) *y Poetas* (poets), as it is called, begins around 10:00 PM (more or less) and could go on until 2:00 AM. It is held one flight up on the first floor. There is a fee of 13 *pesos* that includes one beverage.

Pan y Arte Resto Bar
Boedo 880 (Bo. Boedo)
Tel: 4957-6702

On a Saturday afternoon I sat at the outdoor café of this little restaurant, listening to the strains of tango music by Piazzolla. On some nights this notable bar offers live theater and/or music.

Velma Café
Gorriti 5520 (Bo. Palermo)
Tel: 4772-4690
http://www.velmacafe.com.ar

This theater-bar (*teatro-bar*) is located in the new popular Hollywood sector of Bo. Palermo. It offers a light menu and drinks to accompany its theatrical and musical productions. The show changes nightly, with some nights featuring tango.

This theater-bar's Web site lists the shows of the month. Dependent on the performer, there is an entrance fee of up to 50 *pesos*.

Theaters *(Teatros)*

Theaters generally feature large orchestras and, when advertised, professional singers and dancers. Tickets for many of these performances can be purchased at discount centers (*carteleras*) on Av Corrientes during the week of the performance for a saving of up to 50 percent. There is one cartelera at Corrientes 1382, locale 24 and another at Corrientes 1660, locale 2.

For many of the listings in this section reservations are essential. Even when theater shows are free, it is often expected that tickets (*boletos*) be picked up at the theater the day before or early on the day of the performance. I once arrived the morning of a performance to get my tickets to a free event, only to find that there were no more tickets available. They had run out (*agotados*) the day before, when distribution began.

Empire
Hipolito Yrigoyen 1934 (Bo Monserrat/Congreso)
Tel: 4953-8254
http://www.teatroempire.blogspot.com

This is a lesser-known theater that occasionally offers tango shows with live music and dance, sometimes free. It dates back to 1934 when it first opened its doors. For the past three years, for a period of about six weeks in the Spring (Oct–Nov), Empire has offered a wonderful free show of live music and dance, entitled *Bacanazo en el Aire*. It traces the history of tango on the radio. The theater gets packed with retired Argentines who are given a chance to relive the era of their youth. The singing, dancing, and orchestral music as well as the video montages and pictures evoke memories for many and inform those of us who did not grow up in this environment about the radio protagonists of tango and the music of that era.

(Teatro) IFT
Boulogne Sur Mer 549 (close to Avs Pueyrredón and Corrientes) (Bo. Once)
Tel: 4962-9420
http://www.teatroift.org.ar/

Periodically this Yiddish theater sponsors tango concerts. The theater is located on the periphery of the Jewish garment district, Barrio Once. Tickets are generally available from the Casa de la Cultura on Av de Mayo 575, Monday–Saturday, 11:00 AM to 6:00 PM.

La Casa del Tango
Guardia Vieja 4049 (near Calle Medrano and Corrientes) (Bo. Almagro)

On the ground floor of this space there is a theater that sponsors chamber-like tango concerts or visiting orchestras at different times during the year. Upstairs La Casa hosts a *peña* two evenings a week (see previous section on tango bars and *peñas*). Check the daily newspapers or the government Web site http://www.cultura.gov.ar/agenda for cultural events under *música*. Tickets for free events should be picked up two hours before show time.

La Casona del Teatro
Corrientes 1975 (Bo. Balvanera)
Tel: 4953-5595

This intimate theater periodically offers theatrical performances with a tango theme, among other theater options. It doubles as a café serving very light fare.

Maipo Club
Esmeralda 449 (Bo. Centro)
Tel: 4322-4882

This is a multiplex but intimate theater for live performances. It has a great deal of tango history and offers a wide variety of performances from variety shows to local plays, many with a tango theme.

ND Ateneo
Paraguay 918 (Bo. Retiro)
Tel: 4328-2888
http://www.ndateneo.com.ar

This is a large theater that sponsors musical events throughout the year. Because of the popularity of the performers, this theater almost always takes out large ads in the papers and posts ads on billboards throughout the city.

Presidente Alvear a.k.a. Teatro Alvear
Corrientes 1659 (Bo. Centro)
Tel: 4373-4245

Until recently, this theater offered a free, weekly mid-day tango concert featuring the official BsAs Tango Orchestra (*Orquesta de Tango de la Ciudad de Buenos Aires*). It still offers inexpensive tango shows at night. Check the local newspaper for current shows or the government Web site www.cultura. gov.ar/agenda for cultural events under *música*.

Teatro Astral
Corrientes 1639
Tel: 4374-5707)

This is yet another Broadway-like theater that sometimes offers tango spectaculars such as the time that Ruben Juarez, a legendary bandeonista, played. (See picture)

Teatro Colón
Calle Libertad 621 (Bo. Centro)
Tel: 4378-7100
http://www.teatrocolon.org.ar

This famous opera house was recently renovated. I once went to a tango concert on December 11th, the Day of the Tango. I was in line for three hours to get my free tickets and I sat in the highest rung among ardent tango fans. This was a unique opportunity for the common people (*pueblo*) to come out and experience tango on its most sacred altar—this grand old opera house. While tango is not offered frequently, every once in a while a special event is announced in the papers.

Teatro Nacional Cervantes
Libertad 815 (corner of Córdoba) (Bo. Centro)
Tel: 4816-4224
http://www.teatrocervantes.gov.ar

This is a beautiful theater with a great deal of history, just one block from Teatro Colón. Periodically, it offers free tango concerts. Check current offerings on their Web site and in the daily newspapers (*diarios*), *La Nación* and *Clarín*. Tickets are distributed for free performances, early on the day of the show.

Cultural Centers *(Centros Culturales)*

Cultural centers (CC) are places that host a variety of cultural events, including tango shows and art and photography exhibits. Some centers also offer classes in tango and other art forms. Since cultural centers have government support, their shows are either free or reasonably priced.

CC Borges
Viamonte 517 (Corner of San Martín; housed within the mall, Galerías Pacífico)
Tel: 5555-5359

The complement of shows offered by this cultural center changes monthly and includes many opportunities to see tango danced and sung on stage for 20 to 30 *pesos*. In addition, there are a number of art and photography galleries that form part of the center. CC Borges is housed in the beautiful upscale mall, Galerías Pacífico, on Calle Florida. The cultural center also hosts the Argentine School of Tango (*Escuela Argentina de Tango*; EAT). One visit to the mall and cultural center will give you the opportunity to shop, visit the tourist kiosk for maps and brochures, see what is playing, view an art exhibit, and pick up the schedule of classes for the EAT.

CC de La Cooperación, Salón Pugliese
Corrientes 1543 (Bo. Centro)
Tel: 5077-8077

This center offers tango concerts on Wednesday nights beginning around 9:30 PM in its intimate auditorium, Salón Pugliese. These tango concerts are reasonably priced and tickets can be purchased in this center's ticket office after 5:00 PM. Other spaces in this complex are dedicated to the theater, films, literary events, lectures on art and social issues, art exhibits, as well as offering workshops in the arts. At the beginning of the month, the center distributes a calendar of events for all of its offerings.

CC General (Gral) San Martín
Sarmiento 1551 (Bo. Centro)
Tel: 4374-1251

This center offers tango classes as well as free tango concerts on Thursdays. Tickets are distributed two hours before performances. It also promotes music and the arts through other venues. A calendar of events is published monthly and available in this center's foyer.

CC Recoleta
Junín 1930 (Bo. Recoleta)
Tel: 4804-7040

http://centroculturalrecoleta.org/ccr-sp/

This cultural center is located next to the famous Recoleta Cemetary and Mausoleum where Evita Peron was buried, and behind the city's largest weekend craft fair. Periodically, the center offers art exhibits and shows that focus on tango. By accessing this center's Web site under the tab *Espectáculos,* you can see its current agenda. However, its repertoire is more diverse and tango offerings are more limited than at other cultural centers. There is a small café, a gift shop, and a bookstore on the premises.

CC Torquato Tasso
Defensa 1575 (Bo. San Telmo)
Tel: 4307-6506

http://www.torquatotasso.com.ar

This cultural center doubles as a *milonga* and a place to study tango on some nights. Most importantly it has weekend concerts drawing top-notch performers, including well-known tango orchestras, musicians, and singers. It is a popular spot for *porteños* who love to listen to tango. The menu is light, tables are small, and the space is tight. Reservations are essential and tickets may be purchased at the theater discount centers on Av Corrientes (1382 or 1660).

Government Buildings Hosting Tango Concerts

The events sponsored by these government offices can usually be found at the government Web sites: http://www.cultura. gov.ar under *Agenda* and then *música* or *danza*, or http:// www.buenosaires.gov.ar/agenda. Alternatively, you can go to the Casa de la Cultura, on Av de Mayo 575 to pick up announcements and see ads posted about upcoming government-sponsored events. Web sites are only in Spanish, but they are well illustrated and organized.

Concerts are generally free. However, tickets may be required. When required, they are usually available at *Casa de la Cultura*, Monday–Saturday, 11:00 AM to 6:00 PM. For many events, seating is available only on a first come, first served basis. Early arrival is advisable to ensure a seat, but especially if you want choice seats.

These buildings are examples of the finest architecture and interior design that flourished when the city was being built. To hear a tango concert in this atmosphere is a very special aesthetic experience. To get a glimpse of the inside of these buildings, go to Av de Mayo where the Casa Rosada is located. Many of these buildings are located in close proximity. Walk inside and ask if they have flyers for upcoming events. Even if there is no flyer available, you will be able to see the interior of these buildings.

Casa de la Cultura, **Salón Dorado** (House of Culture, the Gold Room)
Av de Mayo 575 (Bo. Centro)

Casa de la Provincia de BsAs (House of the Province of Bs As)
Callao 237 (Bo. Centro)
http://www.casaprov.gba.gov.ar

Centro Nacional de la Música (National Center of Music)
México 564 (Bo. San Telmo)

Palacio de la Legislatura (Palace of the Legislature)
Perú 130 (Bo. Monserrat)
http://www.legislatura.gov.ar

Manzana de las Luces (Block of Enlightment)
Perú 294 (Bo. Monserrat)
Tel: 4343-3260

Palacio de Gobierno de la Ciudad de Buenos Aires, Salón Dorado (Palace of the Government of BsAs, The Gold Room)
Bolívar 1 (Bo. Monserrat)
Tel: 4323-9669

Museums/Galleries

There are museums in BsAs where everyone can learn about the culture, traditions and milestones of the Argentine tango in Buenos Aires. They include a number of old residences of tango icons that have been converted into museums.

In addition, one Saturday a year in October or November the city becomes an open museum, offering free entry as well as free transportation on selected lines between participating museums and historical buildings. Last year (2008), more than 122 institutions participated. The popular Night of the Museums *(La Noche de los Museos)* offers free concerts or lectures at all museums, many focused on tango.

This section is organized by *barrio* to afford the reader the ease of visiting contiguous museums in one day.

Museo Casa Carlos Gardel
Jean Jaures 735 (Bo. Abasto)
Tel: 4964-2015/2071
Hours: Daily (except Tuesdays) from 1:00 PM to 6:00 PM

This refurbished house is where Gardel's mother, Berta, lived from 1927 until her death. It was opened as a museum in March 2003. The house has been completely restored. It is a typical house of the *Abasto* district: long and narrow. You will find a collection of objects used by Gardel and history about his collaboration with other songwriters and

musicians. The museum sometimes sponsors musical events that are advertised in-house.

A walk around this *barrio* will give you an understanding of the importance of Carlos Gardel. Buildings are painted with his image and his music. Some of the restored buildings are colorfully decorated with *fileto* scrolling, a decorative art form typical of the turn of the century.

Museo Mundial del Tango (World Tango Museum)
Rivadavia 830, 1ˢᵗ floor (Bo. Monserrat)
Tel: 4345-6967/8
Hours: Monday to Friday, 2:30 PM–7:30 PM (approximately)

The tango historian and poet Horacio Ferrer spearheaded this museum and art gallery. He is also well known for his extensive collaboration with Astor Piazzolla as a poet and lyricist. The *Museo* is part of the more comprehensive *Academia Nacional de Tango,* a tango resource for historians and researchers. Ferrer still presides over the Academy and the museum's special events. Exhibits trace the history of tango music and dance in BsAs. The walls are lined with large paintings/photos of the major tango poets and musicians. The museum also offers free lectures (in Spanish) on aspects of tango history on the first and third Monday of the month at 7:30 PM. At times it includes musical and/or video accompaniment. On birthdays and memorials, testimonials (*homenajes*) are featured, almost always with musical accompaniment.

Quinquela Martín Museum (a.k.a. *Museo de Bellas Artes de la Boca*)
Av Pedro de Mendoza 1835 (Bo. La Boca)
Tel: 4301-1080
Hours: Tuesday to Sunday, 10:00 AM–6:00 PM

This museum and art school for children features the work of Benito Quinquela Martín, the quintessential portrayer of La Boca, at the turn of the century when Italian immigrants and tango permeated the area. His work, however, documented waterfront activity rather than tango. Nevertheless, there are exhibits that share this space, sometimes focused on tango themes. The museum is seconds away from Calle Caminito, the tango street that hosts a daily art fair and a craft fair on weekends. In this area there are many restaurants that provide streetside tango entertainment, shopping alcoves, as well as old tenements (*conventillos*) where tango featured prominently at the turn of the century.

El Rincón de Lucía (Lucía's Corner)
Del Valle Iberlucea 1196 (Bo. La Boca)
Tel: 4302-6945
Hours: Daily from 10:00 AM–6:00 PM

This historical museum dates back to 1876. It is a renovated tenement structure (*conventillo*) that housed many immigrant men who came to BsAs to work just before the turn of the century. It is typical of the way they lived in the late 1800s. It was in these *conventillos* in La Boca where tango had its beginning. This *conventillo* has a small art gallery in one section, and offers guided tours. On this street, as well as on adjoining streets, there are other *conventillos* that have been converted into shopping alcoves.

Museo Manoblanca
Tabare 1371 (Bo. Pompeya)
Tel: 4918-9448
Hours: Monday to Friday, 8:00 AM–11:00 AM and 2:00 PM–5:00 PM

This museum is dedicated to Homero Manzi, one of the most prolific writers of tango poetry. It also includes the history of the district of *Bo. Pompeya* as evident in the photos and artifacts on exhibit. The museum is privately owned and run. It is best to call to be sure the owner will be present.

Museo de la Casa del Teatro a.k.a. *Sala Museo Carlos Gardel*
Av. Santa Fe 1243 (Bo. Retiro)
Tel: 4811-7678

This museum is for dedicated Gardel fans. It is an old-luxury building with a small two-room museum containing some Gardel documents, photos, objects, letters, and clothing. As of 11/09 the museum was closed for renovation.

Palais de Glace
Posada 1725 (Bo. Recoleta)
Tel: 4804-1163
Hours: Tuesday–Sunday, 2:00 PM–8:00 PM

This gallery dates back to 1910. Originally it was built for ice-skating, but soon started hosting tango events that caused protests among the bourgeois elite. Protests subsided as tango gained social acceptance. In the early days of tango, the *Palais de Glace* hosted many famous tango dancers, composers, and musicians. It was declared a national historic monument in 2004. It sometimes offers free tango concerts.

Milongas with Exhibitions

The *milongas* listed below offer dance exhibitions on a regular basis and some also feature live music. While start-up time for the *milongas* may be late (after 11:00 PM), show time is even later, generally after 1:00 PM. Therefore, you will need to get to and from these clubs by radio-taxi or *remis*. The only way to know who is dancing and/or playing on a particular night is through flyers distributed at the locale or in the monthly tango magazines, *El Tangauta*, *BA Tango*, and *La Milonga*, where full-page ads for many of these *milongas* provides an agenda for the month.

Reservations are important at *milongas* that have featured orchestras and/or dancers. While early arrival may get you a seat without a reservation, it cannot be assumed. It is best to make a reservation for show nights, especially if you want a seat near the dance floor for full view of the dancers. Generally, the best seats are held for regular patrons.

Confitería Ideal
Suipacha 384 (Bo. Centro)
Tel: changes every night, depending on the organizer

Their late night *milongas* on the first floor (one flight up) offer live music for dancing on some nights, and exhibition dancing by professionals, teachers, and well-known *milongueros*, even more often. *Milongas* usually begin after 11:00 PM and shows begin after 1:30 AM. Tango classes sometimes precede the *milonga*. The thrill for me has always been to see the professionals dancing socially among the guests/patrons.

La Viruta
Armenia 1366 (Bo. Palermo)

This is another popular *milonga*, especially with the tango jet set, as well as an after-hours club for old *milongueros*. Thursdays and Fridays feature live music and exhibition dancing.

Porteño & Bailarín
Riobamba 345 (Bo. Centro/ Congreso)
Tel: 4932-5452

This club features a *milonga* and exhibition dancing on Tuesday and Sunday nights. It has gained popularity with old *milongueros* and tourists alike. A class precedes the *milonga*.

Salón Canning
Scalabrini Ortiz 1331 (Bo. Palermo)
Tel: 4832-6753

On Mondays, Tuesdays, and Fridays when *Parakultural* sponsors the *milonga* at Canning, there is a show of either old timers or young dancers. The *milonga* starts at 11:00 PM and the show begins after 1:30 AM. On Thursdays at 10:30 PM, the *milonga* and show is sponsored by *Rouge,* and on Saturday by yet another organizer. Group classes precede all of Canning's late night *milongas.*

On the Outskirts (But worth the trip!!!)

La Baldosa,
Ramón L. Falcón 2750 (Bo. Flores) (near Rivadavia 7200)
Tel: 4601-7988
http://www.labaldosatango.com.ar

The Friday night *milonga* at *La Baldosa* begins at 10:30 PM. It always offers exhibition dancing and sometimes even live music. Its shows are always advertised in the monthly tango magazines. There is a class offered right before the *milonga* beginning at 8:30 PM.

Sunderland
Lugones 3161 (Bo. Urquiza)
Tel: 4541-9776

This gym becomes a dance hall on Saturdays. Exhibition dancing can be seen every Saturday at this historic weekly *milonga.* The *milonga* begins after 10:00 PM when early birds come to eat. The real dancing begins closer to 11:00 PM, and the show is closer to 1:00 AM. It is famous for attracting old timers and tourists from all over the world.

TANGO IN THE MEDIA

I remember the thrill of seeing live, albeit on TV, historical footage of the tango legends—the musicians, orchestra leaders, and singers that had become so familiar to me on the dance floor. They included: Miguel Caló, Juan Darienzo, Anibal Troilo, and Piazzolla among the musicians and orchestra leaders. Among the singers were Angel Vargas and Alberto Castillo. I watched the old movies of Gardel, as well as instructional videos of Carlos Gavito teaching tango, and Pepito Avellaneda doing a *milonga*. I heard interviews with *milongueros* talking about the codes (*códigos*) of behavior and dress that they grew up with, and the dilution of those standards.

In the process, I also found my Spanish skills enhanced. As noted in my introduction, I lived in BsAs for almost a year with the goal of becoming fluent in the language I had heard as a child, but that I could not speak with nativelike fluency. Through the media, I accustomed my ear to Spanish.

Television, especially, is a great tool to enhance your Spanish skills since it offers visual clues to what is being spoken. You may even find an old English-speaking movie that is dubbed in Spanish with English subtitles, another way to reinforce your Spanish and to extend your vocabulary and understanding of the spoken language. News coverage of events with which you are familiar in English is yet another tool to help you improve your Spanish.

The stations listed here are dedicated tango stations. They help you learn more about tango as they move your Spanish forward.

Television
Cablevisión: Channel 505, *Canal Solo Tango* (http://www. tangocity.com). This station features tango interviews, documentaries, concerts, and classes with old masters.

Radio

92.7 FM (*dos por Cuatro*) (two by four) Tango is played on this radio station twenty-four hours a day. Cultural events of the day are announced sometime during their morning programming.

ENTERTAINMENT GLOSSARY IN TRANSLATION

Daily newspapers	*Diarios*
Entertainment section	*Espectáculos*
Discount ticket houses	*Carteleras*
Dinner show	*Cena show*
Theater	*Teatro*
Historic bar	*Bar notable*
Theater bar	*Teatro bar*
Cultural Centers	*Centros Culturales*
Museums	*Museos*
Guided Tours	*Visitas Guiádas*
Concerts	*Conciertos*
Open mike	*Micrófono abierto/ Peña*
Dance	*Bailes/ Danzas*
Music	*Música*
Television	*La televisión*
Radio	*La radio*
Cover charge	*Cubierto*
Minimum	*Mínimo*
Consumption	*Consumición*
Drinks	*Copas*
Entrance fee	*Entrada*
Free	*Libre y gratuita*
Tickets	*Boletos*
Flyers	*Volantes*
Sold out	*Agotados*

Days of the Week

Monday	*Lunes (Lun)*
Tuesday	*Martes (Mart)*
Wednesday	*Miércoles (Miér)*
Thursday	*Jueves (Juev)*
Friday	*Viernes (Vier)*
Saturday	*Sábado (Sáb)*
Sunday	*Domingo (Dgo)*

A CLOSING NOTE

Tango is a bloodline for the economy of Buenos Aires. As is obvious from this chapter, it is available throughout the city twenty-four hours a day and seven days a week. Take advantage of the many ways that *porteños* and *milongueros* were nursed on tango. Allow the music to seep into your veins, to color your dreams, and to talk to your soul. I guarantee that it will also change your dancing.

MAY THE MUSIC BE YOUR MUSE!

Chapter 6
Shopping for Tango

On my first trip to BsAs I had to buy an extra piece of luggage just for the CDs I had purchased. There were so many new orchestras, singers, and music from different eras to which I was exposed. I wanted to add them all to my collection. Moreover, the cost of a CD was about $5, a bargain I could not pass up. The possibilities were endless and the selection made me dizzy. On a subsequent trip, I accumulated enough shoes in nine months that made it necessary for me to mail most of them back home. While mail service was costly, it would have cost more to buy those shoes in the States. Besides, I would never have found the styles and colors I was sending home.

I will admit that I am a self-proclaimed shopaholic. When I first arrived in BsAs I visited every tango shoe store I could find. Many carried their own line of shoes, customized them upon request, and even had their own line of dance outfits. The speciality clothing I found was a bit expensive in these shops. Even though I love to shop, I don't like to overpay. In fact, I pride myself in scouting out bargains. And so I searched out small stores in unlikely places, ones that did not cater to tango aficionados. I would always look for unique garments or pieces of jewelry that had the potential for drawing the attention of *milongueros*, and the admiration of other women. I also love the challenge of taking an ordinary garment and personalizing it with some form of embellishment, many of which I found in craft fairs, antique fairs, and specialized accessory shops.

Every walk in every neighborhood gave me a chance to shop. Shopping malls and galleries abounded. But what drew my attention were neighborhood shops. Dancing in the late afternoon made possible afternoon shopping strolls right before a *milonga*. I always allowed myself time to walk around the neighborhood and look into stores that offered something to the tango aficionado, albeit unwittingly. Over the course of many trips to BsAs, I have discovered inexpensive clothing stores that sold clothing suited for tango, or accessories that helped me personalize garments I had purchased. In addition, throughout the city there are seamstresses that alter or make clothing very reasonably, and shoemakers that fix, stretch, or alter shoes. Given the monetary exchange rate, there is no reason not to buy.

While shopping can be a form of entertainment for women, men also have options that would be costly back home, but are relative bargains in BsAs. They include custom-made suits and shoes. In addition, almost all shoe stores offer men a ready-made selection.

OVERVIEW

The goal of this chapter is to share with the reader what I discovered on my long stays in BsAs, as far as purchasing goods related to tango—from music and books to clothing, shoes, jewelry, antiques, leather, and accessories. In addition, the chapter will discuss briefly the services that dancers might seek out, from shoe repair to clothing alterations and tailor-made clothes.

Throughout the city there are neighborhoods that specialize in different goods. As for music, there are specific streets and strips within *El Centro* where you can buy anything from sheet music and CDs to musical instruments, as well as historical and instructional DVDs. To help in the purchase of

CDs I have provided the reader with a short list of the most popular tango orchestras that are consistently played in the *milongas* of BsAs.

For clothing, there is a wholesale garment district that sells outer wear (*ropa*) and underwear (*ropa interior*), fabric (*tela*), and clothing accessories (*accesorios*), such as notions, sequins (*lentejuela*) and beads (*semillas*). There are also neighborhoods and stretches of blocks dedicated to yarn (*hilo*) and leather (*cuero*), as well as jewelry (*joyas*). In some of these neighborhoods, goods are sold wholesale and craft vendors buy their materials.

In addition, the chapter will list, by *barrio*, shoe stores that cater to tango, and wholesale and retail shops that sell clothing suited for tango.

Weekends (*fines de semana*) in BsAs are for craft lovers and antique collectors. In the different *barrios* you will find many craft fairs (*ferias de artesanos*) that sell unique and handmade garments, jewelry, and accessories that are ideal for tango. There are also antique fairs (*ferias de antiguedades*) and antique stores for which the *barrio* of San Telmo is noted. Here again, there are items such as gloves, old jewelry, hair ornaments, or vintage clothing, which are perfect tango adornments. All will be covered in this chapter.

In many cases, I have provided the reader with directions for accessing listings by public transportation. The chapter ends with a glossary of terms, in translation that should be helpful for shopping in general, but especially for shopping for clothing and shoes.

WHAT TO BUY AND WHERE TO GET IT

Music, Books, and Videos

•**Zivals** (Av Callao 395) (http://www.tangostore.com) and **Musimundo** (Av Corrientes 1753)

These are two large media stores with extensive collections of tango CDs. They are located one block away from each other. The selection at Zivals will make your heart flutter. In addition, at Zival's you can listen to the first forty-five seconds of CD selections before you decide to purchase. There are headphone stations throughout the store. In November 2008, I paid 21 *pesos* for a CD with twenty tangos, the equivalent at that time of $7. Zivals's Web site sells CDs online, as well as VHS tapes and DVDs. Music can be listened to before purchasing, and once purchased it can be shipped worldwide. The store also has a healthy collection of books related to tango.

In buying videotapes or DVDs, be sure to check on the formatting. Ask whether they are formatted for PAL or NTSC. Generally, U.S. playback machines are calibrated to play only NTSC format. But PAL is the preferred format in Argentina. There are many instructional tango tapes, as well as tourist guides for BsAs that make wonderful gifts, provided they can be viewed on the playback machines back home.

Directions: *Subte* Line B to *Callao* station

•Calle Florida and Calle Lavalle

Florida and *Lavalle* are intersecting streets that are also pedestrian malls in the heart of the downtown-shopping district. Both streets are lined with small independent businesses. Many stores on Lavalle, in particular, sell CDs and DVDs at good prices. I especially like the selection at Lavalle 582. The owner is extremely well versed in the tango genre. He also has an extensive collection of instructional tapes and old Gardel movies *(películas)* available in DVD format. Again don't forget to ask if the movie is formatted for PAL or for NTSC.

Directions: *Subte* Line C to *Lavalle*

•Kiosks throughout the city

There is a tango kiosk (*kiosco*) on Av Corrientes at the corner of Parana. It carries books (*libros*), CDs, magazines (*revistas*), and trinkets related to tango. In addition, there are kiosks on most corners of BsAs that sell not just the daily newspaper and magazines, but promotional (*ofertas*) CDs and books. For example, I bought a tango series that featured a different tango musician or singer every month. It included a CD together with a small hardcover book about the life and work of the featured artist.

• **Bookstores *(librerías)* all along Av Corrientes** from the *Obelisco* on Av 9 de Julio up to Av Calloa.

Many bookstores on this strip carry instructional VHS tapes and DVDs. In addition, some host book signings, recitals, and performances by tango musicians and singers.
Directions: *Subte* Line B to *Callao* station

- **Librería Gandhi** (Corrientes 1743) is one such store. It doubles as a cultural center (*Casona del Arte)* with an in-house theater and café. It often features tango performers and also offers tango classes. Over the years, it has served as a meeting spot for literary figures and intellectuals. It is a good source for books on tango. You can check online at http://casonadelarte.com.ar/Principal.htm for a current monthly calendar.

- In all the bookstores that line Av Corrientes, you will find books of tango lyrics (*letras de tango*), usually on stalls in the front of the store. Some authors to look for are Hector Angel Benedetti, Jose Gobello, Eduardo Romano, and Juan Angel Russo. Because they are written in Spanish, you either need to be able to read the language or use a dictionary to help you decipher the meaning. Understanding the lyrics will help you appreciate the sentiment behind tangos. *Milongueros* will tell you that for some, lyrics inspire their dancing. Personally, I feel I dance with greater sentiment and intensity when I know the lyrics or at least the story behind a particular tango.

- **Tango sheet music (*partituras*) and instruments**
  - **Calle Talcahuano**
    The four blocks between *Avs Rivadavia* and *Corrientes* are dedicated to music and musical instruments.
    Directions: *Subte* Line A to *Lima* or Line B to *Uruguay*

  - **Antigua Casa Nuñez**, Sarmiento 1573 (http://www.antiguacasanunez.com)
    Casa Nuñez is known for its collection of classical guitars (*guitarras*). Pictures of famous guitarists, including Gardel, are displayed in the store. It also sells tango music. Classes are offered with the purchase of a guitar. The 1500 block of Sarmiento has a number of other music stores.
    Directions: *Subte* line B to *Uruguay*

- **CDs sold at *milongas***
  When you hear a tango you like at a *milonga*, speak to the DJ to find out whose tango it is (*¿De quién es el tango?*), or what it is called (*¿Cómo se llama?*). Some DJs have compiled the most popular tangos, *milongas*, and tango-waltzes, and sell CDs of danceable music at the *milongas* rather reasonably.

- **Popular traditional orchestras** whose music is frequently played at *milongas* include:
  - Rodolfo Biagi

- Miguel Caló
- Francisco Canaro
- Alberto Castillo
- Angel D'Agostino
- Juan D'Arienzo
- Alfredo De Angelis
- Carlos Di Sarli
- Osvaldo Fresedo
- Osvaldo Pugliese
- Enrique Rodriguez
- Ricardo Tanturi
- Anibal Troilo
- Hector Varela, and
- Angel Vargas, the singer, among many, many, many others

Clothing

The city is replete with many small clothing stores that offer possibilities for dancing tango. There are upscale, self-contained shopping malls, semi-enclosed galleries of small privately owned shops under a single address, and lots of smaller stores and boutiques scattered around the city. For the traveler looking for a one of-a-kind option, there are showrooms and private residences that have been converted into selling space. In addition, for the budget-minded traveler there are wholesale/retail stores that also offer clothing options suited for tango.

I have isolated a few areas of the city that I got to know personally and, therefore, could recommend. Clothing stores are not limited to the shops, malls, and sections of the city that I have highlighted here. In fact, there are very few areas of the city that do not cater to shoppers. Generally speaking, you can find many shops in and around most *subte* stations.

This section will start with the higher end shops that cater to tango clothing, followed by the shopping malls, shopping strips, and finally ending with the wholesale/retail shopping district, *Barrio Once*. In all cases don't be afraid to ask if there is a discount for paying with cash (*¿Hay descuento si pago al contado?*).

- **Shops and Designers with a Dedicated Line of Tango Clothing (*Ropa de tango*)**

  This is a very small sampling of shops and showrooms that specialize in tango clothing. Others can be found advertised in the tango magazines *BA Tango, Tangauta*, and *La Milonga*.

  - **Tango Imagen:** Anchorena 606 (Tel: 4864-3847) This boutique is located in the heart of *Bo. Abasto*, a block from the *Abasto* shopping mall. The owner, Maria Jazmín, individually beads her clothing line. Her designs and her beadwork are exquisite.
    Directions: *Subte* Line B to *Gardel* station

  - **Tango Moda:** *Av de Mayo* 1370, 16th floor (Tel: 4381-4049) Tango clothing and accessories for both men and women are featured. Hours fluctuate but are advertised as Monday–Friday 1:00 PM–8:00 PM and Saturdays 11:00 AM–2:00 PM.
    Directions: *Subte* Line A to *Saenz Peña*

  - **Berretines de Bacana:** (Tel: 4334-8484) (http://www.berretinesdebacana.com.ar) I met the designer of this business at a tango festival in BsAs. Since she did not have on display exactly what I wanted, she suggested I go to her studio in San Telmo. I purchased a beautiful hand-crocheted jacket in wine. While it has been a few years since that purchase, I recently logged on to her Web site and was quite impressed with the designs on their homepage. The site is under construction so full access is not available. However, the designer advertises *pilchas milongueras* (milonguera clothing) and *vestuario para espectáculos* (costumes for shows).

- **Mimi Pinzón:** Venezuela 3502 (Tel: 4932-0946) (http://www.mimipinzon.com.ar/) This showroom specializes in tango garments made to order.
  Directions: *Subte* Line A to *Castro Barros* followed by a healthy walk

In addition, clothing for tango is sold at many stores that sell tango shoes. They are listed in this chapter under "Shoe Stores by Neighborhood." Additional stores that sell clothing for women can be found in the following malls, streets, and/ or neighborhoods:

• **Shopping Malls**

Malls in BsAs are like most malls throughout the U.S., consisting of a comprehensive array of stores, ATM machines, and a food court. Some stores carry clothing and accessories suited for tango. In addition, the kiosks in malls are a good place to pick up specialty nylons that constantly need replacement. Multiplex cinemas are also found in some of the malls.

- **Galerías Pacífico:** Calle Florida (800 block) and Av Córdoba (*Bo. Centro*) (http://www.galeriasPacificó. com.ar)
  Directions: *Subte* Line C to *San Martín* station

- **Patio Bullrich:** Av Libertador 750 (*Bo. Recoleta*) (http://www.shoppingbullrich.com.ar)
  Directions: Accessible by taxi or bus

- **Paseo Alcorta:** Salguero 3172 (*Bo. Palermo*) (http:// www.paseoalcorta.com.ar)

Directions: Accessible by taxi or bus

- **Alto Palermo:** Santa Fe 3253 (*Bo. Norte*) (http://www.altopalermo.com.ar)
  Directions: *Subte* Line D to *Bulnes* station

- **Abasto Shopping:** Corrientes 3247 (*Bo. Abasto*) (http://www.abastoshopping.com.ar)
  Directions: *Subte* Line B to *Carlos Gardel* station

• Shopping Strips
- **Av Florida** (Blocks 200 to1000) is a pedestrian mall and a prominent commercial strip. It is filled with stores, galleries, and malls that sell all kinds of clothing (as well as shoes, leather goods, lingerie, books, records, souvenirs, etc). The famous mall *Galerías Pacífico* is located on the 800 block of Florida.
  Directions to Av Florida: *Subte* Line B to *Florida* or Line C to *Lavalle*

- **Av Santa Fe** (1200 to 2900 block) offers fifteen blocks of window-shopping.
  Directions: *Subte* line D to station *Aguero* leaves you near the 2900 block

- **Av Córdoba** (4400 to 4600 block) offers a few lovely small shops that sell tops, skirts, slacks, and dresses that women can easily use for dancing. These blocks are located near Av Scalabrini Ortiz (i.e., near Canning, a *milonga* hot spot).
  Directions: Accessible by bus and taxi

• **Wholesale Garment District**

Barrio Once is the garment district of Buenos Aires, with many wholesale and inexpensive retail stores. Some stores in this *barrio* sell only wholesale (*al por mayor*), while others also sell retail (*al por menor*). They usually charge more for items purchased *al por menor*. For that reason you may see two prices on a garment in a window display. The lower price is the wholesale charge.

The garment district is not limited to the sale of garments or fabric. There are streets dedicated to electronics, watches, and toys, to name a few. For tango shoppers, there are also streets dedicated to skirts (*polleras)*, tops (*remeras, bustiers)*, dressy dresses (*vestidos para salir)*, underwear (*ropa interior)*, and accessories.

The more commercial retail stores in *Barrrio Once* are located on **Av Corrientes**, which is replete with clothing stores from the *Pasteur* station to the *Pueyrredón* station on *subte* Line B. The 2500 block of Corrientes has three shopping galleries, each filled with small dress and accessory stores. They are **Paseo Imperial** (2510), **Galería del Siglo** (2570), and **Galería Vía del Sol** (2582).

Venture down the side streets off both Av Corrientes and Av Pueyrredón. Here you will find some interesting and inexpensive shops. For example, the 2600 and 2700 blocks of **Calle Bartolomé Mitre**, off *Av Pueyrredón*, have a number of stores that specialize in skirts—sometimes just a few styles in a variety of colors. While the quality may not always be great, the choices are varied and the prices are right, especially for an item that looks good and fits well. Unfortunately, the smaller side street stores that sell wholesale and retail do not usually allow you to try on garments. You need to know your taste well and your size (*tamaño)*. For a unique look, you can personalize items with accessories bought at craft fairs.

Other side streets in *Bo. Once* that feature items of interest to tango dancers are:
- Pasteur (400 block) between Av Corrientes and Lavalle – clothing and accessories
- Larrea and Azcuénaga (400 block of both streets) – dressy fabric
- Sarmiento (close to Av Pueyrredón) – lingerie
- Castelli (300 block) – clothing
- Paso (300 block) – clothing

Directions *to Barrio Once*: *Subte* Line A to *Plaza Miserere* or Line B to either *Pasteur* or *Av Pueyrredón* stations

Leather Goods

• **Calle Murillo:** Leather (*cuero*) district with small stores selling bags, shoes, clothing, jackets, belts, etc.
Directions: *Subte* Line B to *Gallardo* station; *porteños* in the neighborhood will point you in the right direction.

In addition, leather liquidators can be found on the following intersecting streets:
• **Calle Venezuela** (1400 block)
• **Calle San Jose** (500 block)
Directions to both: *Subte* Line E to *Independencia* station, followed by a five-block walk

Shoes

Many shoe stores (*calzados, zapaterías*) offer you the option of having your shoes (*zapatos*) made to order (*a la medida*). You can ask them to change colors, leather, heel height (heights range from 5–10 cm), and heel shape. I would advise against special orders unless you love the shoe, and the store allows you to back out of the order if it is not what you expected or does not fit properly. I know many people who were disappointed with the end product or whose order was not ready when promised.

If you decide to special order shoes do not **(I repeat, DO NOT)** wait until the last day of your stay to pick up your shoes. Give yourself at least a week window of opportunity to be sure the shoes fit well and are what you wanted. At the end of this chapter is a vocabulary list related to shoes. It should be helpful if you decide to place a special order for a color, finish, or heel height that is more suited to your taste.

Shoe stores are usually open Monday through Saturday, and closed on Sunday. On Saturdays, they may be open only a few hours, so check their schedule in advance. To check hours of operation you can log on to the Web site that appears next to their name. In addition, almost all tango shoe stores advertise in the tango magazines *BA Tango, El Tangauta*, and *La Milonga*.

While most stores have extensive collections of shoes, some of their shoes may not be on display. Sales people generally go out of their way to help you find something you like. If you don't find what you want in one store, there are many other stores, often on the same block or in the same neighborhood. I have organized the shoe stores by *barrio* and within *barrios*, by street, making it easy to visit a number of stores at one time.

Additionally, many shoe stores have a small selection of clothing, as well as accessories suited for dancing. As expected, they can be a bit overpriced. But if the item is something you really like and it looks good on you, I wouldn't hesitate to buy it. A few stores even offer tango classes on the premises.

- **Barrio Centro (Shoe stores are grouped by street and proximity to each other)**

Calle Esmeralda
- **Mirtha Paulo** – Esmeralda 461 (http://www.mirthapaulo.com.ar)
- **Tango Brujo** – Esmeralda 754 (http://www.tangobrujo.com)

Calle Suipacha
- **Todo Tango** – Suipacha 245, Locale 2
- **Bailarín Porteño** – Suipacha 251
- **Scarpe Mahara** – Suipacha 252 (http://www.scarpemahara@hotmail.com) (smaller selection, but good prices)
- **Centro Artesanal del Tango** - Suipacha 256 (http://www.suipacha256tango.com.ar)
- **Darcos** – Suipacha 259 (http://www.darcostango.com)
- **Flabella** – Suipacha 263 (http://www.flabella.com)

Calle Diagonal Norte
- **Alanis** – Diagonal Norte 936

Calle Sarmiento
- **Aurora Lubiz** – Sarmiento 722, 7th floor (http://www.auroralubizropa.com.ar) (Cell phone: 15-5699-3537); showroom is open Tuesday 2:00 PM–6:00 PM and Saturday 2:00 PM–6:00 PM) Call for appointment
- **NeoTango** – Sarmiento 1938 (http://www.neotangoshoes.com)
- **Tango Leiki** – Sarmiento 1947 (http://www.tangoleike.com)

- **Barrio Retiro**
  - **Comme il Faut** - Arenales 1239 (3M) /tel: 4815-5690 (http://commeilfaut@netizen.com.ar)
  - **Taconeando** – Arenales 1606 (taconeandoshoes.com.ar)
  - **Raquel** – Arenales 1974, 3rd floor (http://www.raquel-shoes.com)
  - **Segunda Generacion** – Esmeralda 1249 (Tel: 4312-7136)

- **Barrio Abasto/ Almagro**
  - **Madreselva** – Av Corrientes 3190 in the Abasto Plaza Hotel (http://www.madreselvazapatos.com.ar)
  - **Artesanal** – Calle Tomás de Anchorena 537 (http://www.shoes-susanaartensanal.com)
  - **Tango 8** – Calle Anchorena 602 (http://www.tango8.com)
  - **Lolo Gerard** – Calle Anchorena 607 (http://www.lologerard.com)

- **Barrio Palermo**
  - **Greta Flora** – Gascon and Guardia Vieja (http://www.tangoshoes@gretaflora.com)

- **Barrio San Telmo**
  - **Delie Shoes** – Piedras 843, corner of Av Independencia (http://www.delieshoes.com.ar)

Jewelry

Calle Libertad (100 – 300 block) three blocks between Av Rivadavia and Av Corrientes where old and new jewelry is sold – mostly 18k gold and good quality silver.
Directions: Subte Line A to Lima or Line B to Carlos Pellegrini

Antiques

Every Sunday from 10:00 AM to 6:00 PM there is an **antique fair** (*Feria de Antiguedades*) at **Plaza Dorrego** (Calle Humberto Primo, corner of Defensa) in San Telmo. This open-air market and pedestrian mall is a **MUST**. The entire area for at least 6 blocks is closed to traffic. There are many street vendors and small antique shops that are open for business. The area features all kinds of antiques, including music, old vinyl records, jewelry, fans, gloves, and vintage clothing. One wing of the fair is dedicated to tango art, photos, and artifacts, specifically Calle Humberto Primo 450–500. In addition, there are tango dance and music exhibitions scattered throughout the fair. The most popular exhibition is presented by *El Indio,* a longtime local favorite dancer and teacher. At the end of the day there is an outdoor *milonga* right on the plaza.
Directions: Accessible by bus

In Bo. Abasto, **El Cambalache del Abasto** (*Calle Anchorena* 585) is a small antique store that has a nice collection of collectables related to tango including books and sheet music. This store is surrounded by a number of good tango shoe stores on one side of the street and the Abasto Mall on the opposite side of the street.
Directions: *Subte* Line B to *Carlos Gardel* station

Specialty Items

Whenever I travel to BsAs, I make it a point to bring back home, items that I know to be unique. While shopping malls and Argentinean chain stores such as Zara's, Ted Bodin's, or Había Una Vez have a good selection, what they sell is mass-produced. There is nothing more exhilarating for me than finding a handmade crochet top or skirt, a one-of-a-kind piece of jewelry, or a handknitted, crocheted, or woven shawl or wrap that no one else has. That is what you get at craft fairs, specialty shops, and even yarn shops. For those artisans who also dance tango, there is the possibility of buying, wholesale, accessories that can be added to mass-produced items to personalize them.

- **Crafts Fairs to Buy Accessories (jewelry, crochet tops, bags, etc.)**

There are craft fairs scattered around the city, especially on weekends. The list here is just the tip of the iceberg, but it is a good beginning, especially if your time is limited.

Barrio Recoleta

- *Plaza Francia* is open Saturdays and Sundays from 10:00 AM till around 6:00 PM or 7:00 PM. It is great for gifts and accessories (jewelry, crochet tops, bags, etc.).
  Directions: Accessible by bus or taxi only

Barrios Microcentro, San Telmo, and La Boca

- **Mercado de las Luces**, *Calle* Perú at the corner of Alsina. Monday to Friday 10:00 AM–7:30 PM, and Sundays from 2:00 PM–7:00 PM
  Directions: *Subte* Line A to *Plaza de Mayo*

- **Paseo de la Resistencia**, Avenida de Mayo 649. Open Monday to Saturday from 10:00 AM–9:00 PM. It sells typical crafts and regional products.
  Directions: *Subte* Line A to *Perú*)

- **Artesanos para el Tango**, *Avenida* San Juan 410, corner of *Calle* Defensa. (http://www.artesparaeltango.com.ar)
  Directions: Accessible by bus

- **Calle Caminito in La Boca** is good for artwork and photos around the tango theme.

Directions: No *subte* access; many buses end their run at *Calle Caminito*

Barrio Belgrano
-   **Plaza Manuel Belgrano**, *Avenida* Juramento and Vuelta de Obligado. Open Saturday and Sunday from 11:00 AM–8:00 PM
    Directions: *Subte* D to *Juramento*

• Accessories for Embellishment

These are a few good areas of the city for those of you inclined to buy embellishments for personalizing basic unadorned clothing:

-   **Calle Junín** (300 block) in **Bo. Once** between Sarmiento and Corrientes for beads (*semillas*), sequins (*lentejuelas*), and the like.
    Directions: *Subte* Line B to *Pasteur*

-   **Calles Pasteur, Azcuénaga**, and **Larrea** in **Bo. Once** for decorative fabric. There are many small tailoring shops around the city that will adjust clothing or make garments to order (*a la medida*). All you need to do is bring your fabric and a model of the garment, a picture, or a pattern (*molde*).
    Directions: *Subte* Line B to *Pasteur*

-   **Calle Lavalle** in **Bo. Once** offers many wholesale stores that sell decorative notions for sewing and embellishment.
    Directions: *Subte* Line B to *Pasteur*

-   **Calle Scalabrini Ortiz** (900 block) for yarn to crochet, knit, or to weave your own accessories. Classes are sometimes offered for next to nothing.
    Directions: Accessible by bus

In addition, there are yarn/knitting shops around the city that often offer handmade one-of-a-kind accessories suited for tango. For example, I bought hand crocheted scarves, shawls, and wraps at prices that were very reasonable.

SERVICES

Shoe Repair and Dye

There are many shoe repair stores (*compostura de calzados*) throughout BsAs that will do the normal replacement of soles and heels, and that also stretch new shoes, change heels altogether, or replace straps—all of which I have had done.

One such place is centrally located under the *obelisco*, **Apolo XI**. The shoe repairman there has a kiosk in the Av 9 de Julio *subte* station (*Pasaje Obelisco Sur*, Locale 4-6). You should enter the station where Diagonal Norte, Corrientes, and 9 de Julio meet. The kiosk is at the beginning of the commercial underground corridor that enables you to cross Av 9 de Julio underground. There is another kiosk, a few stores down, (locale 18-20) that sells all kinds of dyes (*tintes*) and cleaners for shoes.

Custom-Made Suits

Rocha-Cashmires (Hipolito Yrigoyen 809) is a large store that specializes in tailor-made suits (*trajes a la medida*) for men and women. The entire process is done over a few visits, and the end result is really worth the price. They have their own selection of fabrics, and tailors on the premises.

Clothing Alterations

Every neighborhood has shops that alter clothing (*hace alteraciones o arreglos*) for very reasonable rates. I have had zippers fixed, clothing taken in, or hems taken up. These same shops will sometimes make garments for you following a sample (*modelo/ muestra)*, picture or sketch (*dibujo*), or pattern (*molde*) that you bring them.

GLOSSARY OF SHOPPING TERMS

Shopping Vocabulary

Wholesale	*Ventas al por mayor*
Retail	*Ventas al por menor*
Hand made	*Hecho a mano; artesanal*
Hand crocheted or woven	*Tejido artesanal; crochet*
Cash	*En efectivo/ al contado*
Discount	*Descuento*
Just looking	*Mirando nada más*
Size	*Talle/tamaño*
Where may I try it on?	*¿Dónde se puede medir?*
Number of payments for charging?	*¿Cuántos pago?*

(Generally, when charging, the salesperson will ask you for the number of payments you would like to divide your purchase into. In the United States, the question is never asked because you are automatically charged the entire amount as one payment. The answer in BsAs then is always one payment (*un pago*).)

Clothing Vocabulary

Skirt	*Pollera*
Top	*Remera*
Tank top	*Musculosa*

Slacks, dressy	*Pantalones de salir*
Dress	*Vestido*
Shawls	*Estola; chal*
Short jackets	*Saquitos*
Overcoat	*Sobretodo*
Scarf	*Bufanda*
Bathing suit	*Malla*
Underwear	*Ropa interior*
Bras	*Sostén, corpiño*
Nylons	*Medias*
Accessories	*Accesorios*
Dressy clothing; eveningwear	*Ropa para salir; Ropa de noche*
Clothing for dancing	*Ropa para bailar*
Suit	*Traje*
Tie	*Corbata*
Belt	*Cinturón*

Shoe Vocabulary

Shoes	*Zapatos*
Sandals	*Sandalias*
Sneaker shoes	*Zapatillas*
Open toe	*Punta abierta*
Closed toe	*Punta cerrada*
High heels	*Taco alto*
Medium heels	*Taco mediano*
Straps	*Tiras*
Polish	*Betún*
Shoe brush	*Cepillo para los zapatos*
Laces	*Cordones*

Colors and Finishes

Black	*Negro*
White	*Blanco*
Gray	*Gris*
Brown	*Marrón*
Red	*Rojo*
Blue	*Azul*
Green	*Verde*
Wine	*Vino; Bordó*
Gold	*Dorado*
Silver	*Plata*
Copper	*Cobre*
Metallic	*Metalizado*
Stamped design	*Grabado*
Leather	*Cuero*
Suede	*Gamuza*
Patent leather	*Charol*

Jewelry Vocabulary

Jewelry	*Prendas; joyas*
Rings	*Anillos*
Earrings	*Aretes; pantallas*
Necklaces	*Collares*

A CLOSING NOTE

Shopping for tango in Buenos Aires is a sport, and a great diversion. Certainly there are many places throughout the city where shoe shopping alone could consume both a great deal of time and money. The selection of both stores and shoes is mindboggling.

But there are also opportunities to shop for clothing, leather, accessories, vintage clothing, antiques, and handcrafted garments and jewelry. There are neighborhoods with block after block of well-priced gold and silver jewelry, leather goods, CDs and DVDs, music and instruments, as well as books. For the do-it-yourselfer, there are concentrated areas where fabric, beads, sequins, yarn, and other forms of creating and personalizing your clothing can be found.

Shoes can be custom-made, as can men's suits and women's clothing, for much less than you would pay back home. In addition, alterations to clothing and to shoes can be made easily, and very inexpensively. Buenos Aires provides the tango aficionada with an opportunity to augment their tango wardrobe (as if you don't have enough), while bringing back home a usable and personal souvenir, and maybe even setting a trend.

Enjoy the indoor malls, galleries, and boutiques. But also enjoy the outdoor courtyards, craft fairs, antique fairs, and street and *subte* vendors. I have even enjoyed shopping in the *milongas*. Some of them allow the DJ to sell CDs, or provide space for established shoe stores to set up shop. They may even give the bathroom attendant the right to sell clothing to the patrons. You would be surprised at the places where tango goods are available.

This truly is a city that reeks with tango! And with the exchange rate, there is no excuse for not buying. It is your opportunity to give back to tango and Buenos Aires what it has given you. Besides, if you don't buy what you love, you will regret it when you get back home and can't find what you saw in Buenos Aires, and at the price you saw it.

JUST GO FOR IT!

Chapter 7
Tango Resources by Barrio

As I traveled to early evening *milongas*, usually by public transportation, I would walk in and around the various *barrios*. I noticed that each *barrio* had its own flavor and characteristics, and some even had their own style of dancing tango. I explored neighborhoods that had a great deal of tango history and noted tango resources that the untrained eye might miss. Invariably, I would come across some business that fed my tango frenzy: stores that sold shoes, interesting jewelry and clothing, and other accessories that I found useful for tango, even if the storeowner had not purchased his stock with that intention. I found restaurants that offered tango shows, or simply played tango as a backdrop to dinner, as well as schools and studios for tango. They have been described in detail in the appropriate chapters. Chapter 2 reviewed restaurants; Chapter 3 talked about tango schools and studios; Chapter 4 focused on dance halls and clubs; Chapter 5 covered other venues for tango entertainment; and finally, Chapter 6 focused on shopping options.

OVERVIEW

This chapter is intended to save the reader valuable time by bringing together all the tango resources that are listed in this book and organizing them by neighborhood. In doing so, the

163

reader is able to take an afternoon to explore all that is related to tango within a single *barrio*. Shopping, collecting flyers for shows, eating, listening to music, learning about tango history, seeing the places where tango lived and breathed in another era, and even dancing all become one seamless activity. That is, if you have the stamina to do it all—back to back to back.

For purposes of this chapter, the city has been divided into twelve areas. Each area represents a single *barrio* or, in some cases, two contiguous *barrios*, when tango resources are sparse within just one. Because *El Centro* is the largest area with the greatest number of tango resources, I have split it into two zones: Lower *Centro* and Upper *Centro*. I have also split *Balvanera/Bo. Once* into three zones because it encompasses many resources over a large terrain.

Each *barrio* or set of *barrios* begins with a short description, giving the reader an overview and flavor of the area. Within each *barrio*, **street names appear in bold print,** and under each street are the businesses, *milongas*, studios, dance schools, clubs, bars, restaurants, theaters, museums, concert halls, and cultural centers with their **street number in parentheses**. In some cases, an entire block (e.g., 200 block) or series of blocks (e.g. blocks 001–300) is referenced because it/they cater to a particular product, as is the case with music stores on *Calle* Talcahuana, book stores on Av Corrientes, and jewelry stores on *Calle* Libertad. The nature of the establishment is identified, e.g., shoe store, *milonga*, museum. Finally, the entry ends with the chapter of the book (in parentheses) in which there is a complete description of the listing.

One way of getting to know tango neighborhoods and tango history more intimately is by taking advantage of guided walking tours. Since they usually cater to Spanish speakers, knowledge of spoken Spanish is a requirement. However, if you want to improve your Spanish listening skills guided walks are a step in the right direction. Some walking tours related to tango are described within the barrios that sponsor them or at the end of the chapter under Guided Walking Tours.

SELECTED *BARRIOS* OF BUENOS AIRES

1. Barrio Centro (Microcentro and San Nicolás)

Description of *Barrio*

Contrary to its name, *El Centro* is not the center of the city, but it is in many ways the heart of the city. It is alternatively referred to by English guidebooks as downtown BsAs.

The *Obelisco* is its most prominent icon. Two main thoroughfares, *Av 9 de Julio* and *Av Corrientes,* intersect at the *Obelisco.*

El Centro is one of the main commercial areas of BsAs. It houses the financial district of the city at the lower end, as well as the theater district and the famous opera house, *Teatro Colón,* at the upper end. In addition, you will find small clubs, restaurants, and galleries scattered throughout. Some blocks are dedicated to the sale of specific items, such as jewelry, tango shoes, music, and leather. Most importantly for tango aficionados, some of the most popular *milongas,* schools of tango, and studios are located in *El Centro.*

Two intersecting streets, *Calles Florida* and *Lavalle,* are pedestrian malls (*peatonales*) closed to commercial traffic. Businesses on these streets and in the surrounding area run the gamut from high-end shops and department stores to small businesses selling clothing, lingerie, leather goods, shoes, books, tango CDs, instructional DVDs, and tango souvenirs.

Av Corrientes runs the length of *El Centro* and it is the lifeline of the theater district. Here you will find many movie houses, theaters, and concert halls, as well as restaurants and bookstores.

In *El Centro*, you will see a cross-section of the population of BsAs. This includes well-dressed businessmen and women, and tourists from around the world. At the other end of the financial spectrum, you will also see beggars, homeless families, and paper pickers (*cartoneros*). The streets also bustle with street vendors and performers, and the *subte* system bustles with musicians. Many of these performers live off tango. Be prepared with small change for the entertainers, especially if you plan on taking pictures or videotaping.

Because the area covered by *El Centro* is dense and full of many tango resources, I have divided it into two sections, **Lower *Centro*** and **Upper *Centro***.

1A. LOWER CENTRO (Lies east of Av 9 de Julio. Served by *subte* Lines B, C, and D)

Resources by Street (address appears in parentheses next to the establishment)

- **Av Rivadavia**
  Museo Mundial de Tango (830) – Museum (Ch 5)

- **Sarmiento**
  Nuevo Estudio La Esquina (722) – Dance school, 4th floor (Ch 3)

Aurora Lubiz (722) – Clothing, 7th floor (Ch 6)

- **Lavalle (pedestrian mall [*peatonal*])**

  (Blocks 500 – 800) – CD stores in abundance (Ch 6)

  Tango's (582) – CD and DVD store (Ch 6)

  Lavalle and Florida – Tango exhibition dancing at this intersection

  Los Inmortales (746) – Restaurant (Ch 2)

- **Viamonte**

  Centro Cultural Borges (517) – Cultural center with theaters and exhibits (Ch 5)

  Escuela Argentina de Tango (517) – School of Tango (Ch 3)

- **Florida (pedestrian mall (*peatonal*))**

  Corner of Bartolomé Mitre (100) – Tourist information center (Ch 1)

  Piazzola Tango (165, basement) – *Cena* show (Ch 2)

  (Blocks 200 to 1000) – Stores and shopping galleries (Ch 5)

  Galerías Pacífico (800 block, corner of Viamonte) – Shopping mall (Ch 6)

- **Maipu**

  Plaza Bohemia (444) – *Milonga* (Ch 4)

- **Esmeralda**

  Teatro Maipo (443) – Theater (Ch 5)

  Mirtha Paulo (461) – Shoe store (Ch 6)

  Tango Brujo (754) – Clothing and shoe store (Ch 6)

- **Suipacha**
  Todo Tango (245) – Shoe store (Ch 6)
  SAM (251) – Shoe store (Ch 6)
  Scarpe Mahara (252) – Shoe store (Ch 6)
  Centro Artesanal del Tango (256) – Shoe store (Ch 6)
  Darcos (259) – Shoe store (Ch 6)
  Flabella (263) – Shoe store (Ch 6)
  Confitería Ideal (384) – *Milonga, practica,* restaurant, and shows (Ch 2, 3, 4, 5)
  BA Tango Shop (453) – Tango souvenirs (Ch 6)

- **Diagonal Norte**
  Alanis (936) – Shoe store (Ch 6)

- **Av 9 de Julio**
  El Obelisco (corner of Av Corrientes) – Structural icon of Buenos Aires

1B. UPPER CENTRO (Lies west of Av 9 de Julio. Served by *subte* Line B)

- **Av Corrientes (Theater district of BsAs)**
  El Vesuvio Confitería (1181) – Ice cream parlor with a weekly tango show (Ch 2)
  El Vesuvio Resto Cultural (1187) – Restaurant-theater (Ch 2)
  Los Inmortales (1369) – Restaurant (Ch 2)
  Cartelero (Galería 1382, local 24) - Discount tickets for shows (Ch 2, 5)
  Kiosco de tango (corner of Parana) – Tango newsstand (Ch 6)
  Blocks 1500–1800 – Many CD, DVD, and bookstores (Ch 6)

Teatro San Martín (1530) – Theater complex (Ch 5)
Centro Cultural de La Cooperación (1543) – Cultural center, *Sala Pugliese* (Ch 5)
Cartelero (1660) – Discount tickets for shows (Ch 2, 5)
Teatro Astral (1639) – Theater (Ch 5)
Teatro Presidente Alvear (1659) – Concert hall (Ch 5)
Musimundo (1753) – CD and DVD store (Ch 6)
Librería Gandhi (1743) – Bookstore, café, in-house theater (Ch 6)

- **Sarmiento**

  Multiple guitar stores (1500 block) – (Ch 6)
  Centro Cultural General San Martín (1551) – Cultural center (Ch 5)
  Antigua Casa Nuñez (1573) – Guitar store (Ch 6)
  Chiquilín (1599) – Restaurant (Ch 2)

- **Bartolomé Mitre**

  El Arranque (1759) – *Milonga* (Ch 4)

- **Av Rivadavia**

  Bien Porteño (1392) – Tango bar and restaurant with shows (Ch 2, 3, 4, and 5)

- **Cerrito (runs parallel to and adjoining 9 de Julio)**
  Tango Porteño (570) – *Cena* show (Ch 2)

- **Libertad**

  (Blocks 001–400) – Jewelry stores from Av Rivadavia to Corrientes (Ch 6)

> *Teatro Colón* (621) – Opera house and concert hall (Ch 5)
> *Teatro Nacional de Cervantes* (815) – Concert hall (Ch 5)

- **Talcahuano**
  (Blocks 001 – 400) Music stores from Av Rivadavia to Corrientes (Ch 6)

- **Montevideo**
  Lalo's (353) – Restaurant (Ch 2)
  Pepito's (383) – Restaurant (Ch 2)

- **Av Callao**
  Casa de la Provincia de BsAs (237) – Government building; concerts (Ch 5)
  Zival's (395) – CD and bookstore (Ch 6)

2. Barrio Monserrat a.k.a. Congreso

Description of *Barrio*

Bo. Monserrat is the heart of the historic district and the seat of government. Its main artery is *Av de Mayo*. At one end of this avenue is *La Casa Rosada* (the Pink House), and at the other end is the Congress (*el Congreso*). In between these two structures, and more specifically around the *Casa Rosada*, are beautiful, old, and well-maintained government buildings. Throughout the year many of them offer free concerts and special events connected to tango. The Web site http://www.buenosaires.gov.ar generally lists these events in their calendar (*agenda*).

Bo. Monserrat lies between *El Centro* to the north and San Telmo to the south. It is accessible on *subte* Lines A, C, and E.

- **Av de Mayo**

  El Cabildo (500) – Colónial structure and museum; craft fair in courtyard (Ch 6)

  Casa de la Cultura (575) – Tourist information and theater, *Salón Dorado* (Ch 5)

  Paseo de la Resistencia (649) – Indoor daily craft market (Ch 6)

  Café Tortoni (825) – Restaurant-café and tango shows (Ch 2, 5)

  National Academy of Tango (833) - Tango school (Ch 3)

  Los 36 Billares (1265) – Restaurant with shows (Ch 2)

  Tango Moda (1370) – Clothing store on 16th floor (Ch 6)

- **Hipolito Yrigoyen**

  Rocha Cashmires (809) – Men's tailor-made suits (Ch 6)

  Empire (1934) – Theater (Ch 5)

- **Alsina**

  Mercado de las Luces (intersecting with Perú) – Craft and antique vendors (Ch 6)

- **Venezuela**

  1400 block – Leather liquidators (Ch 6)

- **México**

  Centro Nacional de la Música (564) – Music school and theater (Ch 5)

  Fervido (1314) – Restaurant with shows and *peñas* (Ch 2)

- **Bolivar**

    Palacio Municipal de BsAs (1) – City Hall/
    concerts (Ch 5)

- **Defensa**

    Starting at Av Belgrano – Sunday street craft
    fair and flea market (Ch 6)

- **Perú**

    Palacio de la Legislatura (130) – Government
    building/concerts (Ch 5)
    Manzana de las Luces (294) – Historical
    building/theater and crafts (Ch 5, 6)

- **San Jose**

    Chiqué at *Casa Galicia* (224) – *Milonga* (Ch
    4)
    500 block – Leather liquidators (Ch 6)
    Café Montserrat (524) – Restaurant/ bar with
    shows (Ch 2, 5)

3. Barrios San Telmo and Constitución

Description of *Barrios*

The *barrios of San Telmo* and *Constitución* lie next to each
other with Av 9 de Julio separating them. While some of
their buildings are well maintained and even restored, many
are run down and in need of rehabilitation. However, this
mix of buildings is what gives these *barrios* their charm and
provides evidence of their antiquity. These *barrios* are also very
popular among tourists, as well as the younger set looking for
inexpensive restaurants, lots of character, and an animated
nightlife.

    San Telmo differentiates itself because it has a great deal
of tango history. Some refer to it as the "old quarters." It
is a treat walking through its cobblestone streets, in and out

of old churches, and into very old buildings converted into restaurants, some with interior courtyards. Many of these buildings are maintained as beautiful old relics of another era, while others show their age and their neglect.

San Telmo is the home of many artists and artisans, as well as antique shops, historical market places, art galleries, intimate clubs, and tango dinner-shows. It is also the home of the most famous antique fair (*feria de antiguedades*) and flea market at Plaza Dorrego. On Sundays, the surrounding streets are closed off to traffic to allow all kinds of vendors, artisans, musicians and dancers to take to the streets. Many of them are dedicated to tango. In addition, there are a number of craft fairs (*ferias de artesanos*) within a small radius.

Barrios San Telmo and *Constitución* lie between *Bo. Monserrat* to the north and La Boca to the south. They are accessible on *subte* Lines C and E.

- **Balcarce**

    La Ventana (431) – *Cena* show (Ch 2)
    Michelangelo (433) – *Cena* show (Ch 2)
    El Viejo Almacén (799) – *Cena* show (Ch 2)

- **Defensa**

    Antique Fair on Sundays (corner of Humberto Primo at Plaza Dorrego) – (Ch 6)

> *Torquato Tasso* (1575) – Cultural center, shows, *milongas*, classes (Ch 3, 4, 5)

- **Perú**
  > *El Querandí* (302) – *Cena* show (Ch 2)

- **Piedras**
  > Delie (843) – Shoe store (Ch 6)

- **Chile**
  > *La Cumparsita* (302) – Restaurant with shows (Ch 2)

- **Pasaje (Alley) Giufra**
  > *La Scala de San Telmo* (37) – Theater (Ch 5)
  > Between *Calles* Defensa and Balcarce – Sunday craft fair (Ch 6)

- **Estados Unidos**
  > *Bar Sur* (299) – Restaurant-bar with shows (Ch 2)
  > *Candilejas* (1500) – *Cena* show (Ch 2)

- **Humberto Primo:**
  > *El Balcón de la Plaza* (461) – Restaurant and shows (Ch 2, 5)
  > 400 block on Sundays – Tango art and artifacts sold by street vendors (Ch 5)
  > *Centro Región Leonesa* (1462) – *Milonga* (Ch 4)
  > *Lo de Celia* (1783) – *Milonga* (Ch 4)

- **Av Juan de Garay**
  > *La Casona de Fernando* (2301) – Restaurants with shows (Ch 2)

4. Barrio La Boca

Description of *Barrio*

La Boca lies at the southernmost part of BsAs. It has a great deal of history and it is truly the cradle of tango. It was the port of entry for Italian immigrants at the turn of the century, many of whom lived in old tenements, referred to as *conventillos*. By and large, *conventillos* have been converted to shopping alcoves, museums, theaters, and restaurants. Some still function as housing units. The architecture of *La Boca* has not changed much over the years, with the exception of the addition of a great deal of color. It remains a very poor neighborhood, and an artist colony where struggling artists and artisans maintain studios, galleries, and living quarters. *La Boca* hosts tourists from around the world, and holds a daily art fair and a weekend craft fair.

The tourist walking area is lined with inexpensive restaurants and street dancers trying to draw visitors into local cafés and restaurants. *La Boca* also houses the museum of Quinquella, an artist who is the quintessential depicter of life in this *barrio* during the early years of the twentieth century.

As I walked off the beaten path on to quieter streets, I was warned by the local police to be extra careful. Walking on the beaten path during daytime hours is quite safe. The streets are brimming with visitors, buses, vendors, and local police.

175

Nevertheless, it is a good idea to keep money and identification close to your chest. It is also advisable to carry small bills to pay for food, service, merchandise, and transportation, since vendors are usually low on small bills and change.

Door-to-door cab service is highly recommended for safety when going to the area's *cena* shows at night. Again, ask your driver in advance for the cost of the ride and be sure to have the exact amount ready.

La Boca lies at the southernmost point of BsAs, past *San Telmo*. It is accessible only by bus, with a number of bus lines completing their run at the main attraction, *Calle Caminito* at the waterfront (*Riachuelo*).

- **Caminito**
  By the waterfront (*Riachuelo*) – Cafés; tango street performers; arts and crafts (Ch 6)

- **Del Valle Iberlucea**
  El Rincón de Lucía (1196) – Historic conventillo and museum (Ch 5)

- **Av Pedro de Mendoza**
  Museo de la Boca Benito Quinquela Martin (1835) – Museum (Ch 5)

- **Vieytes**
  Señor Tango (1655) – *Cena* show (Ch 2)

5. Barrio Balvanera a.k.a. Once

Description of *Barrio*

Balvanera is a sprawling working class neighborhood. It houses the wholesale and garment district, making it a good option for the value minded shopper or the do-it-yourselfer who is intent on saving money on jewelry, fabric, lingerie, accessories, and notions. Here, fabrics of all kinds and colors are available at bargain prices, together with button stores, trim and notions for sewing, and clothing wholesalers. A few very well regarded *milongas* are also found in this area, as well as restaurants and theaters that feature tango shows.

Balvanera was the former hub of Jewish life and the port of entry for many Russian Jews at the turn of the century. Where Jewish shop owners and residents once were the predominant inhabitants, today Koreans and Catholic Argentines have moved onto the scene.

This *barrio* begins where *El Centro* ends, at Av Callao/Entre Rios, and it extends past Av Pueyrredón. It is accessible on *subte* Lines A, B, D, and H. Line H, the newest addition to the underground transportation system, is expected to run the length of Av Pueyrredón once construction is complete.

For ease of travel, I have divided *Balvanera* into three zones:
- South side of Rivadavia
- North side of Rivadavia
- The wholesale shopping district

5A. South of Rivadavia

• **Av Rivadavia**

> *Café de los Angelitos* (2100) – Restaurant and nightly *cena* show (Ch 2)

• **Hipolito Yrigoyen**

> *Empire* (1934) – Theater (Ch 5)

• **Matheu**

> *Parrilla Bravo* (24) – Restaurant with tango ambiance (Ch 2)

5B. North of Rivadavia

- **Avenida Callao**
  Casa de la Provincia de Buenos Aires (237) – Government building; theater (Ch 5)
  Zival's (395) – CD and DVD store (Ch 6)

- **Sarmiento**
  Neo tango (1938) – Shoe store (Ch 6)
  Tango Leiki (1947) – Shoe store (Ch 6)

- **Riobamba**
  Porteño and Bailarín (345) – *Milonga* and classes (Ch 3, 4)
  El Beso (416) – *Milonga* and classes (Ch 3, 4)

- **Av Corrientes**
  La Casona del Teatro (1975) – Theater (Ch 5)
  Estudio DNI Tango (2140) – Dance studio (Ch 3)

5C. Garment District and Wholesale/Retail shopping Area

- **Junín**
  300 block – Wholesale bead stores for jewelry making and decorating (Ch 6)

- **Pasteur**
  400 block – Clothing and accessories (Ch 6)

- **Azcuénaga**
  400 block – Dressy fabric (Ch 6)

- **Larrea**
  400 block – Dressy fabric (Ch 6)

- **Lavalle**

  2100 block – Sewing notions and decorative accessories (Ch 6)

- **Paso and Castelli**

  200–400 blocks – Wholesale and retail shops; clothing and lingerie (Ch 6)

- **Bartolomé Mitre**

  2600–2700 blocks – Wholesale and retail shops; skirts, dressy slacks, tops (Ch 6)

- **General JD Peron**

  Sabor a Tango (2535) – *Cena* show (Ch 2)

- **Sarmiento**

  2500–2700 blocks – Lingerie shops (Ch 6)

- **Corrientes**

  2500 block – Shopping galleries; small stores with dressy garments (Ch 6)

6. Barrio Abasto

Description of *Barrio*

The *subte* Line B station *Carlos Gardel* leaves you in the heart *Bo. Abasto*, a working class neighborhood. Because of its connection to Carlos Gardel, the legendary tango singer, *Bo. Abasto* is replete with many tango stores, images, and resources. The station also happens to be part of the lower level of the *Abasto* shopping mall.

Across the street from the mall on *Calle Anchorena* are numerous tango shoe stores and tango memorabilia shops. The Gardel museum (the refurbished home where Gardel's mother lived in the late 1920s and 1930s) is about two blocks from the train station. Walking in this neighborhood, you will see many buildings that have been painted with tango sheet music, images of Gardel, and with *filete*, a decorative art form that flourished during the turn of the century

There is a delightful walking tour of *Abasto* on Saturdays. The streets become the stage, with local residents reenacting life during the turn of the century. The tour guide also provides a bit of history about Gardel and tango. The guided walk starts at the *Abasto* Plaza Hotel on Av Corrientes, walks you through the Gardel Museum, and ends at the *Amaycha Bar*, a tango café that doubles as a restaurant and school for teaching *canyengue* tango.

The line of demarcation between *Bo Abasto* and it neighbor *barrios Balvanera* and *Almagro* are imprecise. *Abasto* is accessible via *subte* Line B that runs the length of Av Corrientes.

- **Boulogne Sur Mer**
  Teatro IFT (549) – Theater (Ch 5)

- **Av Corrientes**
  Madreselvas at Abasto Plaza Hotel (3190) – Shoe store (Ch 6)
  Abasto Shopping Center (3247) – Mall (Ch 6)

- **Anchorena**
  Artesanal (537) – Shoe store (Ch 6)

Regiónales del Abasto (557) – Tango souvenirs (Ch 6)

Tango Escuela Carlos Copello (575) – Tango school/studio (Ch 3)

El Cambalache del Abasto (585) – Antiques and tango collectables (Ch 6)

Tango 8 (602) – Shoe store (Ch 6)

Tango Imagen (606) – Clothing store (Ch 6)

Lolo Gerard (607) – Shoe store (Ch 6)

Amaycha Bar (628–632) – Bar-café; *canyengue* tango classes (Ch 5)

- **Jean Jaures**
  Museo Casa Carlos Gardel (735) – Museum (Ch 5)

- **Guardia Vieja.**
  La Casa del Tango (4049) – Tango and poetry *peñas* (Ch 5)

- **Pasaje Carlos Gardel (Carlos Gardel alley)**
  Esquina Carlos Gardel (3200, Corner of Anchorena) – *Cena* show (Ch 2)

7. Barrio Almagro

Description of *Barrio*

Almagro, while limited in tango resources in comparison to the other *barrios* already discussed, has some resources that should not be missed. It also is a working class neighborhood. On Saturdays there is a farmer's market in *Plaza Almagro*. Across the street from the plaza is a very intimate and old tango bar, *Boliche de Roberto*. It still serves as a hangout for musicians and aficionados of tango. It is not for the faint of heart, but it is a must for anyone who wants to see the intensity with which the younger generation and the locals listen to this music.

The line of demarcation between *Bo. Almagro* and its neighbor, *Bo. Abasto*, is imprecise. On some maps the two *barrios* are undifferentiated. Parts of *Almagro* are accessible via *subte* Line A.

- **Bulnes**

  Boliche de Roberto (331) – Bar and *peñas* (Ch 5)

- **Rivadavia**

  Confitería Las Violetas (3899) – Restaurant and coffee house (Ch 2)

- **Venezuela**

  Mimi Pinzón (3502) – Tango clothing and accessories (Ch 6)

- **La Rioja**

  Club Gricel (1180) – *Milonga*, classes (Ch 3, 4)

8. Barrio Boedo

Description of *Barrio*

Boedo has a great deal of tango history and, given its relatively small size, contains a number of good tango resources. This is the *barrio* that is associated with Pugliese, the pianist, composer, and orchestra leader, as well as Homero Manzi, the poet and prolific writer of tango lyrics. Both men made a permanent mark here as evidenced by the restaurants named after each of them. New *milongas* crop up in this area frequently, but do not always last. However, Boedo tango is a recent addition to the *milonga* scene that has become very popular on Wednesday nights.

Boedo sidewalk cafés have a character all their own. On a sunny day, pigeons perch themselves on empty tables and seatbacks. Men come to the tables offering to shine your shoes, while you wait to be served. Historic plaques on buildings and restaurants along Av Boedo (in and around Av San Juan) document the history of this *barrio* and its connection to tango.

Boedo is also the heart of the leather district for artisans and shoemakers. It is where they go to buy, not just leather, but accessories used in the adornment of shoes, belts, and jewelry. This is not a district for window-shopping, but for serious leather artisans. I went with the intention of buying leather and a buckle for a belt I wanted to have made. It was for me an adventure and a challenge to negotiate in Spanish for goods that I could not name. Nevertheless, it was a lot of fun.

Boedo is flanked by *Barrio Almagro* to the north and is accessible via *subte* Line E.

- **Av San Juan**
  Boedo Tango (3330) – *Milonga* (Ch 4)
  Esquina Homero Manzi (3601) – Restaurant and *cena* show (Ch 2)
  Maria del Sur (3645) –Clothing shop (Ch 6)
  Maria Canal (3655) – Clothing shop (Ch 6)

- **Carlos Calvo**
  La Casa de Anibal Troilo (2540) – *Cena* show (Ch 2)

- **Boeda**
  Esquina Osvaldo Pugliese (909) – Restaurant with shows (Ch 2, 5)
  Pan y Arte Teatro (876) – Theater (Ch 5)

> *Pan y Arte Resto Bar* (880) – Restaurant-bar
> with music (Ch 2, 5)
> 1300–1600 blocks – Leather district (raw
> materials) (Ch 6)

• **Sanchez de Loria**
> *Bien Bohemio Café Cultural* (745) – Coffee
> shop; tango shows and *peñas* (Ch 5)

9. Barrio Retiro

Description of *Barrio*

El Retiro is a relatively small *barrio*. It is the home of *Estación Retiro*, the bus and train terminal that transports passengers north of the city and to outlying cities throughout Argentina. It also includes some luxury hotels and modern office buildings.

El Retiro lies between *El Centro* and *Recoleta*, the *barrio* to be described next. It is partially accessible via *subte* Line C. The demarcation between *El Retiro* and *Recoleta* is imprecise. It changes depending on the map that is consulted.

• **Esmeralda**
> *Segunda Generacion* (1249) – Shoe store and
> clothing (Ch 6)

• **Paraguay**
> *ND Ateneo* (918) – Theater (Ch 5)
> *La Esquina de Anibal Troilo* (1500) –
> Restaurant (Ch 2)

• **M.T. Alvear**
> *La Biblioteca Café* (1155) – Restaurant-bar
> with shows (Ch 2)

• **Arenales**
> *Comme il Faut* (1239) – Shoe store (Ch 6)

Taconeando (1606) – Shoe store (Ch 6)

Raquel (1974) – Shoe store (Ch 6)

• **Libertador**

Patio Bullrich (750) – Shopping mall (Ch 6)

10. Barrio Recoleta/Barrio Norte

Description of *Barrio*

Recoleta and *Barrio Norte* are upscale residential and commercial *barrios* that sit side by side. The lines of demarcation between them are imprecise. One main thoroughfare, *Av Santa Fe*, is associated more with *Barrio Norte*. This avenue is lined with shopping galleries and small retail stores, providing a great opportunity for window-shopping. Boutiques are found on the quiet and residential side streets that intersect with Santa Fe. The other main thoroughfare, *Av del Libertador*, is associated more with *Recoleta*. Along this tree-lined boulevard are elegant old European-style mansions, museums, and consulates that date back to the turn of the century. This area is beautifully maintained and manicured.

The *Recoleta* Cemetary/Mausoleum, where Evita Peron was buried, is the dominant landmark in Recoleta. On weekends, the area around the mausoleum becomes one large craft fair. Vendors, artisans, and entertainers sprawl out over the sloped lawns, while hoards of tourists stroll among the kiosks or visit the adjoining cultural center or the shopping mall, BA Design. Restaurants and outdoor cafés border the park area and invite weary and hungry travelers to sit outside and watch tourists and locals enjoy a weekend out with family and friends.

Parts of *Barrio Norte* are accessible via *subte* Line D that runs along Av Santa Fe. On the other hand, what is recognized traditionally as *Recoleta* is accessible only by bus or by taxi.

- **Talcahuano**

  Escuela Argentina de Tango (1052) – Tango school (Ch 3)

- **Av Callao**

  Clásica y Moderna (892) – Restaurant-bar with shows (Ch 2, 5)

- **Av Santa Fe**

  800 – 2900 blocks – Good window-shopping (Ch 6)

  Sala Museo Carlos Gardel (1243) – Museum (Ch 5)

- **Av Pueyrredón**

  Mora Godoy *Tango Escuela* (1090) – Tango school/ studio (Ch 3)

- **Paseo Recoleta (near Recoleta Cemetary)**

  Plaza Francia - Best craft fair of BsAs held every Saturday and Sunday (Ch 6)

  Centro Cultural Recoleta (Junín 1930) – Cultural Center (Ch 5)

- **Posadas**

  Palais de Glace (1725) – Exhibition center and theater (Ch 5)

11. Palermo (Viejo, Soho and Hollywood)

Description of *Barrio*

Barrio Palermo is spread out over a large area. The area closest to the waterfront is noted for its upscale high-rise buildings, old and beautifully maintained residences, museums, parks, and gardens. It is also the home of the famous racetrack that Gardel visited, *El Hipódromo*, which is sung about in a number of tangos (eg. *Por Una Cabeza* – (Losing "By a Head"). The parks and upscale homes in *Viejo Palermo* are found along its widest boulevards, *Av del Libertador* and *Av Figueroa Alcorta*.

The interior sections of *Palermo* have been going through a revival, resulting in smaller subsections where the younger set and locals enjoy an animated nightlife with outdoor cafés, intimate restaurants, pubs, small theaters, and music in the streets. The NY Times referred to it as "the hippest part of Buenos Aires" (2/4/2007). Small garages, bakeries, and town houses have been converted into boutiques, small hotels, and galleries. Narrow cobblestone streets and alleys dotted with old mansions still characterize both *Palermo Soho* and *Palermo Hollywood*.

Most parts of *Palermo* are accessible only by bus or taxi. A small strip is accessible on *subte* Line D that runs under Av Santa Fe.

- **Salguero**
  Paseo Alcorta (3172) – Shopping mall (Ch 6)

- **Av Santa Fe**
  Alto Palermo Shopping (3253) – Shopping mall (Ch 6)

- **Scalabrini Ortiz**
  Salón Canning (1331) – *Milongas*, classes, shows (Ch 3, 4, 5)

- **Armenia**
  La Viruta (1366) – *Milongas*, classes, live music (Ch 3, 4, 5)

- **Gorriti**
  Velma Café (5520) – Club and shows (Ch 5)

- **Cabrera**
  Café Homero (4946) – Restaurant-bar with shows (Ch 5)

- **Córdoba**
  4400–4600 blocks – Women's clothing (Ch 6)
  El Motivo (5064) – *Milonga* and classes (Ch 3, 4)

- **Acuña de Figueroa**
  Greta Flora (1612) – Shoe store (Ch 6)

12. Villa Urquiza

Description of *Barrio*

Villa Urquiza lies outside of the capital district. However, it is a must for tango lovers, since it sponsors two of the oldest and most respected *milongas* of BsAs. Access to either *milonga* requires you to take a radio-taxi or *remis*. This *barrio* is identified with the Urquiza style of dancing tango.

- **Lugones**
  Sunderland (3161) – *Milonga* and show (Ch 4, 5)

- **Av Jose Tamborini**
  Sin Rumbo (6157) – *Milonga* (Ch 4)

SHORT TANGO CULTURAL DAY TRIP

Cementerio de la Chacarita (in ***Barrio Chacarita***) is the mausoleum where Carlos Gardel, the most beloved tango singer and guitarist, was buried and where he is immortalized. On June 25th the area fills with admirers who are there to pay homage to their idol. The mausoleum, a scaled-down city, also has a section dedicated to some great tango figures, including Carlos DiSarli, Osvaldo Pugliese, Anibal Troilo, and Agustín

Magaldi. There are life-size statues of each of them. Chacarita is accessible on *subte* Line B, the *Federico Lacroze* station.

Burial site of Anibal Troilo

GUIDED WALKING TOURS

If you enjoy touring independently, be sure to pick up a local map (*un mapa*) of the *barrio* you are visiting as soon as you get there. Many *barrios* publish their own map and they are usually available at *barrio* restaurants, businesses, and shopping centers. Ask the owner for a guide (*un guía del barrio*) or map, or go to the information booth at the local mall. These maps were produced to highlight and advertise local businesses. There may even be discount coupons inside.

In addition to the walking tour described under *Barrio Abasto*, there are other tours that are sponsored by the government on a regular basis. They often offer tours of the historic bars (*bares notables*) as well as the government buildings, museums, gardens, and of course, the *barrios*. Log on to http://www.buenosaires.gov.ar/agenda and go to "*visitas guiádas.*"

A third option is a tour conducted by the well-known historian, Eduardo Lazzari. He organizes historic walks focused on individual *barrios*, historic streets, specific themes, or famous historical structures. They are offered every weekend and on some weekdays. Some are even offered at night. All are in Spanish. This is a great way to challenge your Spanish (if you don't already speak it), while learning something new. I once took a walking tour of the Recoleta Cemetery that talked about Argentina's literary figures that were buried there. A list of the walks is accessible on the Web site http://www.jehba.com.ar, under activities (*actividades)* and guided tours (*visitas guiádas)*. A recent sample entry (2009) reads:

> *Visita guiáda nocturna por San Telmo y Monserrat:*
> *Viernes 1° y sábado 2 de mayo a las 21.*
> *Tema de la recorrida: "Noche de historia y misterio por los barrios de San Telmo y Monserrat."*
> *Punto de encuentro: En la pirámide de Mayo, en la Plaza de Mayo, Av. Rivadavia y Defensa.*
> *Valor de la visita: $20.*

A CLOSING NOTE

The heart and soul of Buenos Aires lies in its *barrios*. There is even a lovely tango-waltz sung by Alberto Castillo that pays homage to the *barrios*. It is entitled *Cien Barrios Porteños* ("One Hundred Argentine Neighborhoods"), where they are all named. His singing of it, until recently when he died, always worked up the audience. There is a sense of identity and pride that locals feel for their *barrio*.

Each *barrio* has characteristics that differentiate it from neighboring *barrios*. Each has its own history, and its own tango haunts. I have shared with the reader those that I discovered while living in and visiting Buenos Aires over many years.

The purpose of this chapter was to encourage readers to explore *barrios* with an eye to discovering their essence and the ways that tango has contributed to their character.

I have walked around neighborhoods, in and out of side streets, sometimes allowing a sign on a store or a notice on a building to stop me. It really was the word tango that stopped me. At times, I was drawn in by the strains of tango music coming out of a doorway. Inside I sometimes discovered another world. It might have been a little out-of-the-way *milonga*, or a makeshift local tango class. At other times, I would read a flyer pasted on a door or a storefront announcing an upcoming tango event or class.

Walk cautiously, but with curiosity, and leave yourself open to new adventures. And remember to always bring your dance shoes. You never know when you will be faced with an unexpected opportunity to dance.

Let your love of tango help you discover new places!

ADDENDUM 1
BIBLIOGRAPHY OF TANGO GUIDES

Complete Guide: Buenos Aires (2008), de Dios Editores, 131 Tacuarí, BsAs Argentina (ISBN 978-987-9445-44-0)

Fodor's Buenos Aires, 1st edition by Fodor's (2008), Random House, Inc (ISBN 978-1-4000-1965-60)

Frommer's Buenos Aires (2007) by Michael Luongo (ISBN 978-0-470-12478-9) Wiley Publishing, Inc. 111 River St. Hoboken, NJ 07030-5774 ($12.23)

Lonely Planet Best of Buenos Aires by Danny Palmerlee, Lonely Planet Publications

Lonely Planet Buenos Aires City Guide (2008) by Sandra Bao Lonely Planet Publications, 150 Linden St, Oakland, CA 94607 ($12.91)

Lonely Planet Buenos Aires Encounter by Terry Carter and Laura Dunston ($9.59)

Moon Handbooks Buenos Aires, 2nd edition (2005), Wayne Bernhardson, Avalon Travel Publishing ($17.95)

The Rough Guide to Buenos Aires 1 by Andrew Benson, Rosalba O'Brien ($12.91)

Time Out Buenos Aires by Editors of *Time Out* (2008) ($13.57)

City Maps

Buenos Aires City Map (Bilingual) (Laminated) by Julian de Dios (English edition) de Dios Editores, 131 Tacuarí, BsAs Argentina

Tango Buenos Aires Map Guide (English edition) by de Dios Editores 131 Tacuarí, BsAs Argentina

Tango Memoir/History

Long After Midnight at the Nino Bien: A Yanqui's Missteps in Argentina by Brian Winter (2007). (ISBN 13: 978-1-58648-370-8) (Not a guide, but a delightful memoir from a man's point of view with coverage of tango history.)

Tango: An Argentine Love Story by Camille Cusumano (2008). (ISBN-13: 978-1-58005-250-4). Seal Press, Berkeley, CA. This memoir is from a woman's point of view.

ADDENDUM 2
SELECTIVE MILONGAS BY DAY AND TIME

MONDAY/ *LUNES*

Time/ *Hora*	*Milonga*	Address / *direccion*	Extras
3:00 – 10:00 PM	*El Arranque @ La Argentina*	Bartolomé Mitre 1759	Class
3:00 – 10:00 PM	*Lunes de Alicia @ La Ideal*	Suipacha 384	Class
7:00 – 1:00 AM	*Mi Refugio @ Ctro Región Leonesa*	Humberto Primo 1462	Class
8:30 – 4:00 AM	*Lunes de Tango @ Gricel's*	La Rioja 1180	Class
10:30 – 3:00 AM	*Shusheta @ Plaza Bohemia*	Maipu 444	Class
11:00 – 4:00 AM	*Parakultural @ Canning*	Scalabrini Ortiz 1331	Class

TUESDAY/ *MARTES*

3:00 – 10:00 PM	*El Arranque @ La Argentina*	Bartolomé Mitre 1759	-
6:30 – 2:00 AM	*Sentimental y Coqueta @ Plaza Bohemia*	Maipu 444	Class
9:00 – 1:00 AM	*Los Chicos @ El Beso*	Riobamba 416	Class
10:00 – 4:00 AM	*Porteño & Bailarín*	Riobamba 345	Class & show
10:30 – 3:00 AM	*La Noche Ideal @ La Ideal*	Suipacha 384	Class

11:00 – 4:00 AM	*Parakultural @ Canning*	Scalabrini Ortiz 1331	Class

WEDNESDAY/ *MIERCOLES*

3:00 – 8:30 PM	*La Matinee @ La Ideal*	Suipacha 384	Class
4:00 – 11:00 PM	*A Puro Tango @ Canning*	Scalabrini Ortiz 1331	Class
6:00 – 12:00 AM	*La Milonga @ Ctro Región Leonesa*	Humberto Primo 1462	-
6:00 – 11:00 AM	*Lo de Celia*	Humberto Primo 1783	-
7:00 – 3:00 PM	*Sueño Porteño @ Boedo Tango*	Av San Juan 3330	-
10:30 – 2:00 PM	*La Bruja @ El Beso*	Riobamba 416	Class
11:00 – 4:00 AM	*La Viruta*	Armenia 1366	Class

THURSDAY/ *JUEVES*

2:00 – 8:30 PM	*Matineé @ La Ideal*	Suipacha 384	Class
3:00 – 10:00 PM	*El Arranque @ La Argentina*	Bartolomé Mitre 1759	-
4:00 – 10:00 PM	*Nuevo Chiqué @ Casa Galicia*	San Jose 224	Class
6:00 – 12:30 AM	*Lujos @ El Beso*	Riobamba 416	-
`6:00 – 1:30	*Rosicler @ Plaza Bohemia*	Maipu 444	-

196

8:00 – 3:00 AM	*La Cachila @ Gricel's*	La Rioja 1180	Class
10:30 – 4:00 AM	*Niño Bien @ Ctro Región Leonesa*	Humberto Primo 1462	Class
10:30 – 4:00 AM	*Tango Ideal @ La Ideal*	Suipacha 384	Class & show
11:00 – 4:00 AM	*Parakultural @ Canning*	Scalabrini Ortiz 1331	Class & show
11:00 – 4:00 AM	*La Viruta*	Armenia 1366	Class & show

FRIDAY/ *VIERNES*

2:00 – 8:30 PM	*El Abrazo @ La Ideal*	Suipacha 384	Class
6:00 – 2:00 AM	*Entre Tango @ Cto Región Leonesa*	Humberto Primo 1462	-
10:00 – 3:30 AM	*Lo de Celia*	Humberto Primo 1783	-
10:00 – 4:00 AM	*Sin Rumbo*	Jose Tamborini 6157	-
10:30 – 5:00 AM	*Club Gricel @ Gricel's*	La Rioja 1180	Class
10:30 – 3:00 AM	*Unitango @ La Ideal*	Suipacha 384	Class & show
10:30 – 3:00 AM	*La Baldosa @ Salón El Pial*	Ramn Falcón 2750	Class & show
11:00 – 4:00 AM	*Parakultural @ Canning*	Scalabrini Ortiz 1331	Class & show

SATURDAY/ *SABADO*

3:00 – 9:00 PM	*El Arranque @ La Argentina*	Bartolomé Mitre 1759	-
4:30 – 10:30 PM	*Los Consagrados @ Ctro Región Leonesa*	Humberto Primo 1462	Class
7:00 – 4:00 PM	*Cachirulo @ Plaza Bohemia*	Maipu 444	-
10:30 – 5:00 AM	*Las* Morochas *@ El Beso*	Riobamba 416	-
11:00 – 4:00 AM	*Club Gricel @ Gricel's*	La Rioja 1180	Class
11:00 – 4:00 AM	*La Viruta*	Armenia 1366	Class & show
11:00 – 4:00	*Lo de Celia*	Humberto Primo 1783	-
11:00 – 3:00 AM	*A Puro Tango @ Canning*	Scalabrini Ortiz 1331	Class & show
11:00 – 4:00	*Sunderland*	Lugones 3161	Show

SUNDAY/ *DOMINGO*

3:00 – 9:00 PM	*Milonga de Paula @ La Ideal*	Suipacha 384	-
6:00 – 12:30 PM	*Lujos @ Plaza Bohemia*	Maipu 444	-
4:00 – 11:00 PM	*A Puro Tango @ Canning*	Scalabrini Ortiz 1331	Class
11:00 – 4:00	*Lo de Celia*	Humberto Primo 1783	-
10:00 – 2:00 AM	*Club Gricel @ Gricel's*	La Rioja 1180	Class

10:00 – 3:00 AM	*Domingos @ El Beso*	Riobamba 416	Class
10:00 – 3:00 AM	*Porteño & Bailarín*	Riobamba 345	Class & show
10:00 – 4:00 AM	*La Viruta*	Armenia 1366	Class & show

ADDENDUM 3
ALPHABETICAL LISTING OF
RECOMMENDED DANCE HALLS

Dance Halls	Address	Days
Boedo Tango	Av San Juan 3330	Wednesdays (Sueño Porteño)
Canning	Scalabrini Ortiz 1331	Mondays–Sundays
Casa de Galicia	San Jose 224 (2nd floor)	Thursdays PM (*Chiqué*)
Centro Región Leonesa	Humberto Primo 1462 (1st floor)	Mondays, Wednesdays–Saturdays
Confitería Ideal	Suipacha 384 (off Corrientes) 1st floor	Mondays–Sundays
El Beso	Riobamba 416 (near Corrientes) (1st floor)	Tuesdays–Thursdays, Saturdays and Sundays
El Pial	Ramón Falcón 2750	Fridays (La Baldosa)
Gricel	La Rioja 1180	Mondays, Thursdays–Sundays
La Viruta	Armenia 1366	Wednesdays–Sundays
Lo De Celia	Humberto Primo 1783 (1st floor)	Wednesdays, Fridays–Sundays

Dance Halls	Address	Days
Plaza Bohemia	Maipu 444 (near Corrientes) (1st floor)	Mondays–Sundays
Porteño and Bailarín	Riobamba 345 (near Corrientes)	Tuesdays and Sundays
Salón La Argentina (Arranque)	Bartolomé Mitre 1759 (Near Callao)	Mondays, Tuesdays, Thursdays, Saturdays
Sin Rumbo	Jose Tamborini 6157	Fridays
Sunderland Club	Lugones 3161	Saturdays

Index

Breinigsville, PA USA
04 May 2010
237362BV00001B/2/P